MW01417222

The opening sentence of Carey Newman's astonishing book reveals its intention: to "awaken the inner poet"—presumably not only its author's own inner poet but also the poet slumbering within the souls of the book's readers. What follows is a volcanic explosion of metaphors that shower luminous sparks of insight, illuminating the mysterious birthing of books, from the author's labor to the midwifery of editors and publishers, to the social context in which academic books make their way in the world. *Mango Tree* is the richly imaginative distillation of all that Newman has learned from his long experience in the publishing world. This is a book to be read slowly and savored: it is whimsical, playful, and—at the same time—a learned and deeply insightful analysis of the magic that conjures books into existence.

—RICHARD B. HAYS, George Washington Professor Emeritus of New Testament, Duke University

Seamlessly blending insightful advice and lyrical finesse, each chapter resonates with the invaluable guidance of a caring mentor whose wisdom has been hard-won. Whether you're an aspiring writer or a seasoned wordsmith, this remarkable book is a must-have companion, inviting you to unlock your creative potential and unleash the power of telling *your* story. Prepare to be captivated by the enchanting prose, and enjoy fruit from *Mango Tree* on your journey to masterful writing.

—MARCIA ALESAN DAWKINS, senior research scientist at Center for Creative Leadership, author of *Clearly Invisible: The Color of Cultural Identity*

Lifts the whole business of writing and publishing onto previously unsuspected levels of hermeneutical sophistication. A cross between a writer's manual and a firework display employing the theoretical and hermeneutical equivalents of tactical nuclear missiles. Read it and weep. Then start writing.

—N. T. WRIGHT, senior research fellow, Wycliffe Hall, Oxford University

On the one hand, thank heavens that a seasoned academic editor in religious studies still cares deeply about the mystery of writing, especially in the humanistic academy where training drums that experience and desire out of a scholar. On the other hand, I am not surprised that the academic editor is Carey Newman, whose ministrations to his authors and his investment in the potential and self-transformative role of their writing mark his vocation. He has never given in to the academy's bent to turn scholarly writing into a utility, a tool, an asset on a curriculum vitae's balance sheet. I need to be reminded of the reasons to write in the humanities. If you do, too, read *Mango Tree*.

—John F. Kutsko, executive director, Atla

Writers struggle to find words, structure, a cohesive line of argumentation, the right genre. Editors commit to keeping writers focused, hungry, productive. Carey Newman brings years of experience in that regard. Writers may seek muses, but they need to love the labor of turning ideas into prose. Craft a good sentence; the inspiration will come. *Mango Tree* is about the craft of writing, with a trove of practical advice and insights, from paragraph structure to the mysteries of publishing houses. But the book provides so much more. It calls, warns, challenges, invites. Aimed at writers seeking to publish—whether newly minted PhDs, seasoned authors, or academics dusting off scholarship lain dormant—*Mango Tree* reawakens passion for ideas inked on the page. Each section exudes wisdom, wit, and erudition. The section titled "Voice" is a *tour de force* on the nature of a book's true audience. But *show* us what good writings is, we writers so often whine. Open *Mango Tree*. Read the preface. Here, Newman displays the gravity of thick description, the captivating arc of emplotment, and how deliciously sensual a lively turn of phrase can be. *Mango Tree* places in our hands a secret gnosis: no matter the topic or genre, all serious writing, even the most erudite, is in its soul an alchemy of poetry.

—Margaret D. Kamitsuka, Francis W. and Lydia L. Davis Professor Emeritus of Religion, Oberlin College

MANGO TREE

MANGO TREE

The Artistry and
Alchemy of Writing

CAREY C. NEWMAN

FRIENDSHIP PRESS

Copyright © 2023 by Carey C. Newman

All rights reserved.

No part of this book may be reproduced or utilized in any form or by any means, electronic or mechanical, or by any information storage and retrieval system, without written permission from the publisher.

Friendship Press
P.O. Box 117
Wyncote, PA 19095

Library of Congress Catalog-in-Publication data available upon request

ISBN (paperback): 978-1-961088-05-4
ISBN (hardcover): 978-1-961088-06-1
ISBN (ebook): 978-1-961088-07-8

Cover design by Savanah N. Landerholm
Interior design by Savanah N. Landerholm

Printed in the United States of America

in memory of
Stephanie Egnotovich
(1946–2009)

CONTENTS

Acknowledgments   *xi*
Preface   *xvii*

Part I
Introduction

§ 1   Reading   3

Part II
Books

§ 2   Ontology   9
§ 3   Genre   13
§ 4   Taxonomy   19
§ 5   Phenomenology   23

Part III
Writing

§ 6   Paragraph   29
§ 7   Voice   33
§ 8   Plot   41
§ 9   Contents   47

Part IV
Writers

| § 10 | Sociology | 51 |
| § 11 | Social Psychology | 55 |

Part V
Publishing

| § 12 | Editors | 63 |
| § 13 | Presses | 65 |

Part VI
Conclusion

| § 14 | Mythology | 71 |

Notes   77

ACKNOWLEDGMENTS

UMBERTO ECO QUIPS that noetic debts get paid one footnote at a time. I will try to settle one or two of my mine right here, as I owe much to many:

To Jennette Brown, for instilling the passion for sentence diagraming—and thus the love of linguistic structure—at a tender age; to Sandy Dubner, without whose patience, kindness, and unmitigated support I would have not survived my teens; to Linda N. Jewell, who first introduced, and inspired by her own practice, scholarly ways (the debt to her unspeakable); to James Bell, for pointing me to Karl Popper and the dark arts of advanced symbolic logic; to Arie Beenhakker, for helping me see how big and connected it all is; to the nameless, faceless grader who placed a "D–" on a substantive paper I had composed, accompanied by the snide, "Great ideas. Terrible writing"—a comment that haunts to this day; to Curtis Vaughan, who, beyond a daily display of intellectual rigor, elevated the idiosyncratic and the cantankerous to essential professional virtues; to Robert B. Sloan, for using a forty-year argument over the relative merits of National vs. American League baseball to teach me how to think, and for his lectures, lectures that still provide the score for much of my life; to Robert Reid, for loving what he knew so fully that we who had the chance to hear him could not help but love it too; to Jim Barcus, for opening the world of literary criticism to me and doing so with the patience and warmth that always attended his shy reserve.

To the esteemed, but fully suspect, members of the Curry Congress and the EWDC, for fortnightly occasions of food that fostered scholarly friendships on two different continents that have lasted for more than four decades; to Curtis Freeman, for his infectious curiosity about the small and seemingly inconsequential; for marrying his life to his scholarship; for his love of single malt and Cuban cigars; and, most of all, for a friendship that has stood the test of time; to Bob Brian, for his wit, his love of language, his BBQ ribs, and for each and every time we visited the wall to whine about the lunacy that engulfed us; to the blessed memory of Don Juel, Alan Segal, Larry Hurtado, a holy trinity of postdoctoral mentors, who, along with David Capes, became the co-founders, charter members, and chief instigators of the EHCC—for all the laughter, all the late nights, and all of the Highland irrigation we managed to disappear; to Martin Hengel, my Doktorgrossvater, for his unrelenting support and for his own resolute embodiment of scholarly excellence (his warnings about the dangers of academic laziness still ring in my ears); to Tom Wright, Richard Hays, Beverly Gaventa, Reinhard Feldmeier, Marianne Meye Thompson, Rob Wall, Paula Fredriksen, Joel Green, and Scot McKnight, my disciplinary colleagues against whose scholarship and lives I have—and still do—measure my own. I know just how lucky I have been.

To Dan Reid and Hans van der Meij, my own editors, for showing me the glories of this accidental profession; to Dan Alshire (and all at the ATS), for a decade of invitations every February to be "the after dinner personality"—talks that, over time, became the precursor to this present book; to Mike Parsons, without whose example I never would have put flesh to the bones of the scholarly dreams I dared to dream; and, then for being the

acknowledgments

best partner in crime for which a press director could ever wish; to my first publishing colleagues—Richard Brown, Dan Braden, Tom Long, Don McKim, Philip Law, Annie McClure, Jennifer Cox, and Bill Falvey—for pulling back the curtain and, with great patience, showing me how publishing works; to those truly faithful commandos who, for nearly two decades, comprised university publishing's Seal Team 6—Diane Smith, Rusty Edwards, Karla Garrett (Smith), Savanah Landerholm, and Billy Collins—for, well, everything: it was such a joy, from start to finish; to Elizabeth Davis, the best boss one could ever hope to have; to my Fortress publishing compatriots—Will Bergkamp, Emily Brower King, Scott Tunseth, Beth Gaede, Yvonne Hawkins, Laura Gifford, Ryan Hemmer, Bethany Dickerson, Adam Bursi—who make every Wednesday morning into something special; to my fellow press directors and publishing colleagues—Patrick Alexander, James Ernest, Donna Shear, Meredith Babb, Trevor Lipscomb, Joerg Persch, Stefan and der Lahr, John Kutsko, Anke Beck, Henning Ziebritski, Kelly Hughes, Lynn Garrett, and Cathy Grossman, for their welcome to the publishing fraternity, their sage advice, and the very best kind of professional friendship.

There's no practical way to thank my students. But if thirty-five years in the classroom, and especially those golden four at PBA, reveal anything it is simply this: an unpayable debt is owed to those who grace the door of a lecture hall. The energy, the imagination, the hope that tumbles in each fall and spring humbles. Not a week goes by that I am not reminded of just how great a gift it was. What is true of students is doubly so with authors. Being the midwife for 800 books over the last three decades places me in unimaginable debt. I learned much from each. From start to finish it has been a fun ride. Forgive me of my many editorial sins, please. If there be wisdom in what follows, then such virtue is occasioned only by the gifts given from author to editor.

Lots of writers write books about writing publishing. Lots. And each repays reading. This book's invite list for the fictional dinner party includes Clayton Carlson, Umberto Eco, Roberto Calasso, Anne Lamott, Annie Dillard, Terry Eagleton, and Wayne Booth. Only one of these have I met in person, and, yet, they have been constant. Such is the power of the book. Each shares an intense, romantic view of writing and an awe of the book's miracle. But theirs is not a naïve view. Their belief in the numenosity of writing and the glories of the book is chiseled and has bite. This book would enjoy their happy company over the meal and several bottles of good wine before it gladly picked up the tab.

I must thank Joe Esposito, himself a man of letters, for encouragement to write in this season of my life. I'm not sure I would have done so without him telling me so directly and emphatically that I must. Thank you, Joe.

My life has been graced by many unexpected relationships. Two, unlikely ones, have enriched my life in ways that transcend the professional. I here record my debt to the mentorship of Ambassadors Ruth Davis and Lyndon Olson.

Various parts of the present volume have been inflicted upon many along the way. I here thank them for being willing to tell me the (sometimes painful) truth: David Lyle Jeffrey, Richard Hays, Tom Wright, Beverly Gaventa, Michael Hyde. A book is lucky to enjoy a first reader, someone who never balks nor tires of reading draft after draft after draft. Fortuna smiled. This book would not have happened without Sonya Shetty Cronin. Sonya, "thank you" seems so paltry, a bit like soggy mushrooms, but I offer it nonetheless.

I heartily thank my publisher, Will Bergkamp, and Marissa Wold Uhrina and Dr. Savanah N. Landerholm for bringing this book into printable shape.

It would be an injustice not to thank the three women in my life: Leanne, Savannah, Eliza—and I can't forget to thank the Wood dog.

acknowledgments

Stephanie Egnotovich was one of my first publishing colleagues. I well remember the day that she and Richard Brown waltzed into that east end Louisville bistro for a lunch interview. They looked like movie stars, and the world of publishing they described to me that day was no less magical than that of tinsel town. Stephanie loved books. Stephanie loved authors. Stephanie loved publishing. And Stephanie loved editing. She read, and re-read, every last word, of every line, of every page, of every book she edited. Nothing escaped her attention. She made every book better; and she made every author better. Her authors swore by her—even if also sometimes at her—and their fealty was expressed by bringing book after book after book back to her. It was a rocky start to our professional relationship, especially because I was so unjustifiably arrogant: I knew so little and understood even less. Stephanie was hard on me. Very. As she should have been. In the end, I came to appreciate both her and her ways. Stephanie's dismissive sandpapering of each of the projects I dared bring forward made me determined, determined to earn her respect. Forcing me to win her trust was Stephanie's way of expressing love. I never, ever would have become an editor without her. Her approval, when it finally came, sustained me in good times and bad. Stephanie was fierce. She clawed her way into being an editor by being resolute and determined. She flourished in a space that was not always welcoming to a woman. She did so because she refused to back down. Stephanie was complicated and often difficult—but she always was worth every second of work and trouble. The sparkle in her eye and that warm smile told the true inner story. It is my deep pleasure to dedicate this book to her, my colleague, the best editor I have ever known, and my friend. May you rest in God, Stephanie. You are missed by all who had the gift of knowing you.

PREFACE

THE SHACK STOOD next to the lumber yard, tucked hard under the canopy of the giant live oak. Shade and Spanish moss hung silently, motionless in the air. The parking lot's lacquered black pavement and its neat yellow lines dissolved into the chalky, crushed shell yawning before the shed. People parked where they wanted, not where they were told. The shack just big enough for the day's mullet, all huddled tight in the warmer. The makeshift counter, hewn of scraps gleaned from next door, sat at an L to the silver top-sliding cooler that housed the Cokes. The rickety floor fan beat time in the corner. In back, the business end of matters, the smoker, with wispy tendrils still swirling toward the sky. The cramped shack inverse in size to aroma. Sharp, distinctive, pungent. No mistaking the shack's why. The mullet split, brined, dried, smoked, stacked, re-folded, to be engulfed in newspaper and carted out the door. The smell spilling from the shack filled the cab of the truck. Arriving early a must. The mullet were gone shortly after noon.

Mullet always hard work. Never a picnic. *Techne*, start to finish. Local knowledge required to find the schools that followed dawn's rising tides into the brackish waters of Allen's Creek. The hand-thrown net, cast in a well-practiced circle by the seasoned, entrapped the skittish mullet. Skill, precision, a bit of luck. The smoking paid homage to alchemy dating back to de Soto. Disputes over how—and how long—the stuff of lore. Tradition, pride, experience. To eat demanded the surgeon's hand. Unwrapped, unfolded, aroma wafting, mouthwatering, the mullet laid open. No knife. No fork. Just fingers, calloused and stained by dirt. Pushing the fore and middle through the rubbery bark rewarded with warm flesh. A delicate pull yielded a mound, pinched with the thumb's aid. Meticulous, methodical, determined. The fish discarded only when picked clean. What slipped onto the newspaper, or the seat of the truck, rescued. Nothing wasted. That good. Its bones, thousands of them, the fish's posthumous revenge. Mullet never surrendered easily. Always treacherous. Fingers pricked, cut. More grim, the boney stowaways inside a morsel. Cheek and tongue and throat all under the same threat. But when bones avoided, then oily, nutty, meaty, savory. The long draw on the cold Coke. More mullet.

The chain link fence separated the shell lot from the backyard. On the other side stood the mango tree. To hop the fence was to land in the garden of another place and time. To hop the fence was to visit the land of magic, where giants roam, where water is wine, and where the impossible grows. Oranges, grapefruit, lemons, limes—plentiful and everywhere. Trees as weeds. Yards dotted. Communal utopia. Their bounty free for gleaning. All welcomed. That mango tree, no exception. Its limbs bowed, laden, heavy. The ones the sun found blushed. Hues of red, yellow, pink— the very colors of imagination. The others shy, having hid their face in the shade, still green with potential. Knowing touch told the story. Soft, plump, fructuous. Two, three, ripe, warm, cradled like kittens. Back over the fence. Dreams in the cab of a truck.

Care to the wind. Mangoes begged it so. The knife's chipped blade, after one swift swipe on the flannel shirt, sliced the skin, making an irregular cube of the mango's natural pyriform. No reason to peel. Reckless, wanton, feverish. Beckoning as abundant.

There were so many, so much. The excess fell to the floorboard. Irresponsible, greedy, wasteful. The flesh varied, pitted, coarse. Vibrant, deep, earthy. Bold, exotic, different. The mango, like warm butter. Decadent, sumptuous. Juice oozing, dripping, from knife, to hands, to shirt, to everywhere. Sticky, tacky. Mango to the mouth. *Eros* at lunch, *Eros* for lunch.

Part I
Introduction

§ 1

READING

THIS BOOK SEEKS to awaken the inner poet. Whether it can remains to be seen. The odds certainly stacked against it, as such stirring proves a tall order. Books rarely make poets of people. Life does that. But roused, the fantastic beckons, and the ordinary never again satisfies. The mundane only triggers deeper discontent, a restlessness about what can be found over the fence. This book more likely finds an earnest welcome with writing already self-conscious, but which also suffers constant ache. The book aspires to disrupt, to prod, to encourage, to grant full permission, to fortify resolve, to bolster. At the same time the book requests forgiveness of writing much further down the path. Such writing smiles knowingly. The book begs patience, even indulgence. It holds no illusions. It knows itself. The book draws upon the innocent belief that all are poets, even and especially the noetic, and all writing is poetry—even and especially the noetic.

The book decries conformity or converts—but neither turns its back to any. All welcome. But fair warning: disappointment awaits those supposing the hunt for writing's Muse a simple matter. Writing pairs life. Writing's habitus mirrors life's complexities. Both life and writing reside just beyond the grasp. But the analogical extends well beyond asymmetrical. Being a poet comes at a cost. Writing demands sacrifice. Capricious readers wooed only by writing authored in a poet's own blood. No true poet can hide behind their words, for poets are their words. Writing's miracle transubstantiates the merely semiotic into the fully symbiotic. Writing meddles with primal mysteries, it strikes a bargain with Fate. But to write opens wide the door of self for all to peer in—just as it is to live. Poets live to write and write to live. They put themselves in, and on, the line. There can be no other.

Readers may be tempted to read this volume left to right, and there's good reason for doing so. There is intention to the book, an arc, sown into its arrangement. While instructive, such fabricated logic beguiles: no book about writing should ever lure its readers into believing that writing's magic can be so easily named. The conceptual, atomistic arrangement of the book belies the truth that writing is messy, ill-shaped, temperamental, and, on its best days, halting and sputtering. The writing life refuses to be organized lockstep or neatly packaged, as the present volume's outline falsely insinuates. There are no steps to writing; and this book presumes no formula. Constant insecurity and chaos rule the writer's world. Writing perpetually teeters on the precipice of failure. There can be no other.

A second strategy proves more matter of fact. Each of the book's sections stand on their own two feet—and thus can be read in any order. If help is needed constructing a table of contents, § 7 might aid. If picking the right press bedevils, § 12 might merit a quick glance. Service, real service, which this book hopes to provide, depends upon the matching of tool to task at just the right moment. While the detailed vagaries of occasion elude this book's grasp, it does behave as a grammar, a distilled potentiality, for when pragmatic need arises. Motivation for writing arises from the desire to provide real help for real problems inherent to the craft.

But the warning issued above still stands: nothing about writing in blood reductive—and this book is not a compilation of handy tips and tricks. This book seeks to break the cycle of writing the same book repeatedly and seeks to accomplish that by disruption. A third, distinct strategy is to begin with the longest sections—§§ 3, 7, 11—so as to feel along the book's perimeter. But it would be wrong to allow these to bound. The longer sections, true enough, foundational and inherently heuristic. Their sustained effort to array writing's many oscillations around a few fixed points is an attempt to ground a bit of writing's madness. But each section's length fails to render a full accounting. Each betrays intrinsic lack, porousness, absence, and such gaps engender suspicion. The long stand in need. Only overlaps among the long sections—and among the smaller ones as well—generates any coherence the book obtains. The juxtaposition of unequally shaped sections, each autonomous yet wanting, funds deliberate retracing. The book cannot help but repeat itself. Repetition, and sometimes outright contradiction, prevails over enchainment. The book's penchant for the arabesque playfully taunts, and then resists, the repeated wish for concatenation.

A word should be said about the notes. The notes orchestral to prose voicing. The notes acknowledge, freely, prose's debts, but equally provide prose's meta-commentary. The prose can, and should, be read without the notes. The notes can, but probably shouldn't, be read without the prose. If the prose mango, the notes mullet. They find themselves together in the cab of the book.

All writing poetry—or at least poetic. Prose sapped of Faerie languishes, page after page of wasteful errand. Destiny never consigned the epistemic to devolved, disinterested, objective, objectifying. Writing by and for the cognoscenti longs to both enlighten and transport, for all writing transcribes the transfigured. Writing, even the most noetic, embodies the uncompromised trinity of logos, ethos, and pathos. The inherent concord among the three fosters the harmony of profit with delight. Such is the mysteriousness of writing. And it is to this end that this book desires to be read.

Part II
Books

§ 2

ONTOLOGY

A MIRACLE. PLAIN and simple.

Miracularity owed to impossibility, not simply to the difficulties that beset realization. The venture much more than overcoming obstacle, frustration, weakness. What's proposed seems doomed from the start. What's proposed meddles with the most elemental of matters: to fashion from the void. Words out of nothing. Formed, ordered. A metaphysical wonder.

But impossibility yields to improbability. It never just appears without a past. There's always a story. Poseidon to Odysseus, so Fate to it. The gods arrayed against it. The single-eyed troubles the trek into being. The journey begins well enough—hope, hunch, obsession—but one whose end shrouded in uncertainty. It lives shadowed, longing for light. Completion ever haunted. It enjoys nary a night of peaceful slumber. All hangs in doubt, as a nightmare, even as the last lines are added. Improbable as impossible.

Gut-wrenching confession—bound and publicized. No vacillating, no equivocating, no hiding. Contrition numbered on every page. Secrets, flaws, failures—indelible, for all to see. No longer under cover. No taking it back. The finality, a terror. Private made public, the suspected declared.

Revelatory, a herald, a harbinger. It calls out. It raises its voice in the streets. It takes a public stand. It tells all it knows to any who listen. It informs, confirms, establishes, invents, builds, strengthens. It confronts, challenges, changes. It disturbs, dismantles, destroys. It begs, then blesses. It broods, then dances. A two-edged sword. Brazen, prodigal, it frolics in a far-country, giving away what can never be purchased. It scours the abyss, searches the heavens. Transcendent. Its shape formalizes a bit of that truth that has always been. Elusive as allusive, but guileless, absent hypocrisy. Innocent, it gives to those who give to it, surrendering Wisdom for time. Fortune favors its readers.

It refuses self-indulgent profusion. Spectacle bedazzles. But the excessive fails. The interminable perpetually lacks. Only fixing shape—assuming a specific corpus—realizes composition. Only by distilling, condensing, indexing. Only by amassing, adding, tending. Moving forward only by working backward. It gathers all that preceded, that which constituted its making, and in the final line converts the repetitive, the iterative, the tentative into the sustained, the assertive, the testament. It says what needs saying and then works closure, pronouncing a benediction, a conferral that renders all *qua* whole. *Fabula. Apologia. Prophetia.*

Partisan. It takes a side. Never objective, despite its every effort to appear so. Never detached, always rooted. Its summing far more than its past or parts. It presses. It puts its readers in its bind. An act of imposition. Blinded narration impossible. It burdens. *Mythos* insists *dianoia*.

Imitation haunts every turn. The soul struggle is to free itself from the specters cast by others. The powers of inclusion compel conformity. Originality corrupted. Concordance confused with duplication, text with pretext. But each singular. Non-repeatable, unique. Each novel. The contingent particulars prompting composition configure the curious shape. A singular act. Originality triumphs over imitation.

    A dance, a romance, a mystery. A terror, a vision, a dream. Fully mortal, fully spirit. Gloriously flawed. It bridges numen to human, ferrying Sophia across the unknown. A sacred act of cultural sapience. Water made wine. A eucharist, an incarnation. Word made print. Pure miracle, plain and simple.

§ 3

GENRE

THREE KINDS ROAM in the land over the fence. Three and only three. Well, almost.

There are those whose properties house. Grand repositories, ideational museums. Archival, cartographic, diagnostic, forensic, synthetic, theoretic. The opulent, the plethoric, the lacquered. The tidy, the circumspect, the stern. The centrifugal, the expansive, the signifying. Few take the self-imposed pledge the pilgrimage requires. Experts for experts—all in gnostic code.

There are those whose properties reshape, refine. Wisdom born of experience. Practical, useful, applicative, pragmatic, illustrative, analogic, expedient, inspirational. Competent, but closed. Hammer to nail. The untested and the seasoned, the apprenticed and credentialed—those who heal, serve, certify, counsel, lead, instruct, consult in search of a more practiced betterment. Guild at its best—for its best.

There are those whose properties enthrall. Captivating, spellbinding, thrilling, amusing, mesmerizing, seductive, playful. To them the masses flock for escape: guilty pleasure, hermeneutical mystery, fantastical suspense, supernal justice, reconstructed past, fabricated future, timeless myth. Printed joy—published mirth.

Now abide these three. Noetic, transformative, affective. Epistemic, performative, peripatetic. Academic, professional, trade. Nouns, verbs, peanuts. Lions, and tigers, and bears. Three and only three. That's it. No more. Compositional befuddlement reduced to three, prix fixe. Or so it seems.

Coded lines blur. Apollonian form a fantasy, as Dionysus makes mixed wine of pure type. They conceive by their wanton generic indiscretion. They woo, mooch, plunder without permission or remorse. The epistemic pilfers the transformative, turning knowledge into prescription. The transformative purloins what amuses, making joy of praxis. The affective conscripts the noetic, allowing delight to be savored in knowing. Some, unicorn rare, meld, mull, decant all three, obtaining an envied consonance—so phenomenal that lists chronicle their fame.

Try as they might, they can never be just one thing. No two alike. Each a calico—the mottled insuring the singular. Composition draws freely upon the full range of generic variables to realize the unique. As many genres as offerings. The more the merrier. Or so it appears.

Generic properties—with their hermeneutical winks and nods—combined, amplified, or subverted in a myriad of ways. The possibilities endless. And tempting. Generic invention crouches at the door, especially for writing habitually confined to cloistered towers. The epistemic longs to break free. It yearns for impact, for impact in dimension. Knowing for knowing's sake alone frustrates, and it judged insufficient by the many minders. Tracing knowing's full arc a wistful must. Knowing, no longer content, thirsts for more. Much more. Persuasion, influence, deference. Impact. Thrice holy impact. The pursuit of such cultural vivacity triggers generic experimentation, tinkering, mucking. The hope of translating the recondite into the vernacular scales to all-consuming obsession. Without diluting rigor, gravity,

Genre 15

technicality, the oft reclusive gnosis comes to covet a composite generic rendering equally suitable for learned consumption and panoptic dissemination. The pressure intense, the burden great. Viral academe, social scholarship. Esteem measured by the opportune binding of precision and fluency, the esoteric made palatable for the demotic.

But lions do not become tigers or bears overnight—nor easily. Genetic engineering always vexed, acutely so for work marked by the prescribed and demanded. For some noesis, no amount of generic enhancement increases potential impact, despite dreamy aspiration. That not all noesis created equal proves a hard lesson for the most determined among the literati. Affectual hopes stymied by subject itself. The epistemic hunt for cultural currency turns into a fool's errand into foreordained frustration. Circulation circumscribed by specialization. Subject so narrow, so buried, no amount of effort rewarded. For other noesis, generic manipulation offers false promise. The infusion of accessibility, novelty, relatability seems simple enough—exotic rhetorical herbs added at writing's end. Success guaranteed. But anarchy, pure generic anarchy. The noble, but novice, attempt by the hobbyist to achieve wide relevance makes an innocent jumble of generic traits. A hodge-podge. The excess of properties, their disordering, their inherent clash, their gross disproportion works the opposite of what is hoped. Generic doctoring ends badly. The mishmash befuddles, maroons, precludes. Generic confusion produces bookish discontent.

Books adhere to in-scripted types for good reason. When a handful of generic properties concentrate, pervade, and persist, when their thick density becomes identifiable and heuristic, when a still malleable but easily recognizable form emerges, when all that comprises a work coheres and aligns, it is then that genre with its many hues and cues forges a near-sacred social contract. The accretion, and then performance, of a concord of properties not only permits the recognition of generic distinctives among the noetic, transformative, the re-creational, but the compression of a proven harmony of generic features equally provides a coded covenant for reading. Genre, hermeneutical type-setting, figures expectation and contentment. Genre vows, and then delivers—by conforming. Noesis gravitates to its generic mean. It conveys its novel contents by established code.

Genre's many ironies sink in slowly. That the lucky, no matter the generic decision, enjoy celebrated triumph confounds. Whatever composed inexplicably succeeds, regardless. It is as if the gods themselves willed it so. The chosen's ability to channel culture's vernacular baffles. Mystery shrouds such charisms, but those so possessed win the acclaim and bask in the affect most lettered so desperately desire—and repeatedly seek. But to abandon the tried and true in the attempt to mimic the inexplicable ignores an ironic fundamental: the Elysian gift of writing trumps all, even genre.

Equal madness that some subjects so timely, so material, that regardless of genre cultural sparks ignite. It is as if the gods themselves willed it so. Of all that drives impact, synchronicity bears the greatest valence and proves the least controllable. The noetic obsession for an opportune subject—to peer deep within and pluck a particular matter from cultural chaos, something whose singular moment is about to crest—is to chase the wind. The involuntary instinct to search for a focus so arresting that none can resist, to track down what's next, ignores a fundamental truth: capricious, disobedient, and unpredictable timing trumps all, even genre.

Coincidence and charism—an unstoppable tandem, seemingly everywhere, but little to be done to conjure either, let alone both. Other paradoxes frustrate: that the amount of time to command one set of generic codes equals the amount of time to master a second contradicts the practiced experience of learned experts. Just as disciplined noetic proficiency has proven to accelerate the acquisition of any other new literacy, so too, surely, the acquired faculties to command the epistemic genre will translate into prompt and effortless fluency in the forms of the performative and the affectual. But this expectation excusable.

Learning a second or third generic language requires—and enacts—complete resocialization, either as a dedicated, fully immersed practitioner or a taciturn public intellectual. Genre and social location go hand in hand. To compose in a second or third genre parallels the concurrent fashioning of a new, liminal identity. The idyllic denizen of academe becomes the professional consultant, a concessionaire who barters what can be known for how it ought to be done; or the wandering cosmopolitan, an intellectual flaneur, far more at home in café than classroom. Both resulting identities merely proximate to the former.

Noetic impact does not derive from generic experimentation. To write in a genre for the many, and not for the noetic few, correlates to obtaining a new identity. Influence is not a fix topically applied. It is expatriation, it is resocialization. The noetic fails by trying to be something it is not. The noetic cannot make a generic square or triangle of a generic circle. It is as frustrating as it is true that noetic impact results by allowing the noetic genre to do its noetic work—to reach the apprenticed, qualified, equally specialized first and, just maybe, solely. Only after passing through genre's narrow first gate does a second, and even a third, come into view. The public celebration of the noetic does not happen because the academic has changed its spots; it occurs because the noetic kept its spot.

Generic irony prevails: only adherence to the epistemic canons permits the noetic to reach beyond itself. It is as if the gods themselves willed it so. Genre cannot be made to forgive all bookish sin. Only curry can do that.

§ 4

TAXONOMY

Placating the deities of genre wins their favor. Athena rewards conformity. Generic tinkering, even for the loftiest of reasons, transgresses bounded lines, angering the heavens. The dreamy hopes of vast noetic impact are realized only by the disciplined honoring of subject's sacred bonds with genre. The vows exchanged between what and how permit the marvel of who to whom. Such rigor bedevils, but blessed be that which obeys, for it shall inherit the earth.

Researcher to researcher: The newly discovered housed in the categorically dedicated and communally recognized. A circumscribed, singular topic mirrored in an undeviating, perspicuous form—monosemic, mononymous. Focused, demarcated, meticulous. Every door, every box. Embedded, rabbinical, partisan. Everyone, everything. Manic. Disparity reigns. The small writ large, and the large, larger still. Potency leveraged into a compressed inward spiral, tension ever ratcheted, argument ever tightening. Method, a quantum physics, so self-consciously applied that research's what in constant danger of being engulfed by research's how. Discovery so totalizing that it insists itself on disclosure. Gain so disproportionately incremental to heft that expended effort threatens to overwhelm the why of origins. Dreams of monopoly, fears of monopsony. But the more delimited the subject, the more robust the method, the more platted the engagement, the more obedient to form, the more likely the glory of the singular to transcend—a cursed noetic irony.

Master to novice: The deliberate, conscientious cashing of proven wisdom, as equally iconic as the meticulously focused, but with diametrical polarity. Introduced, defined, surveyed. Recounted, sorted, compiled. The complex and complicated distilled and refracted. Held at bay—pursuit of fresh discovery, obsession with method, fixation with argument. The individuated suppressed. Measured. The gnomic substituted for the particular, *langue* for *parole*. Duty, even legacy, curries the care lavished upon such quotidian—they the means by which waves of initiates receive first instruction. Essential tool for the rite of passage. Joy, real satisfaction, derived from service. Joy, real satisfaction, derived from being trusted. But the pleasures of service and trust minced and ground with the crassness of business. Big business. Gatekeeper to gatekeeper for gateway. The glossy, glitzy, the neatly and packaged spectacle, tugs hard. Text tailored to spec, refined edition after calibrated edition. 101 translated into bottom line. Nobility inexorably calculated by royalty—an honorable and rewarding noetic vocation.

Peer to peer: Nestled between exhaustive and essential, poised, ever lurking between the newly discovered and already vetted, a brooding generic sufferance, suspended between lumbering argument and tidy summary, begging, just begging for a turn, waits a noetic wonder. Mature, confident. Neither sterile nor didactic, but a pub's back room, a kitchen table, overflowing with the raucous, a give-and-take among a self-selecting, democratic inner ring. Insider to insiders. Colleague to colleagues. An equal to rivals. Shop talk, glorious shop talk. Preferring the indeterminates of

Taxonomy

abduction and hermeneutical frolic to pedestrian deduction and mind-numbing numbered lists. Parsimony, sweet parsimony. Never too much, never too little. Always just right. Apt, eminently apt. Synchronicity and harmony rejoice. Prose judicious, neither spartan nor excessive. Method—present, operational, effectual, but noted, sublimated, tucked away. Scope, commensurate and sufficient. Not every box in every room, but one box and its contents' many entailments. Connection overwriting dissection. Torque uncoiling, significance unwinding. The way of disclosure independent of the act of discovery. Ideas, shorn of rabbinical trappings, run free, tracing their predestined arc. Subject, protagonist of its own narrative; and narrative, the conveyance of *dianoia*—a collegial noetic ministration.

Noetic to professional: Noesis no longer cloistered. Noesis no longer isolated. Noesis no longer confined. Neither insistence upon meticulous dissection nor deference to curated distillation—nor even instigation of clannish conversation. Instead, sapience. A noetic sapience that enlists the merits intrinsic to discovery to ameliorate the inherent woes of practice. Anatomy governed by exigency. Plot shaped by constraint. Design importuned by imperative. Description to analysis to prescription. Praxis to theory to praxis. Problem to solution to reform. Verb to Noun to Verb. A pragmatic concerto. An economic waltz. Academe, the professions—a union not arranged by the heavens. Literati complain of neglect and disrespect; the credentialed of condescension and disrespect. Fields so remote few can harvest both; toil so demanding few can cultivate both. Yet, two as one, two for one. Perceived, persistent lack makes common cause. Noesis craves implication; practice needs remedy—a stubborn noetic reciprocity.

Expert to the curious: A crossing over. A translation. An exchange. No ruse, no gimmick, no illusion. But embodiment, sacrifice, purgation. Specialized competency marshalled, then rendered in cultural *koine*. *Noesis*, traded—musings writ as musement. Lyric re-tuned. Yet, few make the leap. Few jump the ruts. Intensity, no guarantor. Desire, often futile. Bewilderment. The monosomic so deeply entrenched, mired. An epistemic slough of despond. What captivates for years, decades, of little interest outside a qualified few. But, freakish lightning. A unicorn. Inexplicably, the compendious attracts, noetic nectar. No formula, no recipe. Just dumb luck. Dumb luck and the gods. The gods and the possession of a perceived expertise. The gods and ability to channel culture's collective consciousness. The gods and the art of cultural ventriloquism. The gods and benefiting from a little-understood cultural moment, swelling, cresting. The gods and unlearning. The raw, the first order—and with intention—forgotten. A new recital fashioned from discovery, a recital so fluent in civic vernacular that it enchants and charms, transfixes and inspires, educates and heals. Such unlearning and relearning makes for a new identity. New song fashions new singer—a complete noetic transformation.

Generic clarity empowers. Disciplined choice aligns aspiration with ends: researcher to researcher to discover, appraise, conclude; master to novice to characterize, rehearse, classify; peer to peer to interpret, diagnose, extrapolate; expert to professional to analyze, apply, prescribe; authority to the curious to explain, popularize, amuse. Each calibrated. Each trenchant. Each alembic. Each a *rendez-vous*, each *en route*, each a *souvenir*. Each tailored. Each verbal. Each a memory. Discerning selection among the viable alternatives capitalizes upon the predictable affordances inherent to each, allowing precision its day in the sun.

§ 5

PHENOMENOLOGY

THE BOOK MEANS much and little. Everything and nothing. Sway, clout, weight—surrogate, stand in, delegate. Glutted, empty. Assertive, dependent. Activated, ascribed. Alone, intertwined. A signifier begging significance.

Its mercurial intersubjectivity contradicts the stable, the predictable. Little physiognomic disparity among the noetic. Size, shape. Ink, paper. Bindings, boards. Much the same. Dependable homogeneity speaks volumes. Resemblances cue. The mimetic prompts, invoking long prescribed agreements among what, for whom, to what ends. Modest variation marks inside and out. But such plumage, so captivating, merely differentiates one from another and never proves prime to mattering. It can never be reduced to its cover. The semiotic plays elsewhere.

Potentialities ever encircle. Symbolling oozes between signatures. Just how it comes to mean, just what prompts a sense of self, just how metonymy displaces synecdoche, riddles Wisdom. But it does, in panoply, employing its every trick.

It borrows, even as others lend. Read, vetted, placed. Inclusion bequeaths inheritance. Front-listing grants backing. Warranting by proxy. The almighty power of the colophon. Chosen and catalogued singular from among the many who hoped; arrayed among the select—yet another, in a galaxy of the many. But confederation with consociates initiates the rites of determination. Read, reviewed, placed. Scrutinized, compared. Its lexicon of synonyms and antonyms works the magic of semiosis. The paradigmatic capitalizes on already assessed assignations. The new known by the existing. But appraisal ever a threat to collegiality, and thus annual gatherings become a mass of orchestrated masquerades.

Temporal alignment equally fashions inference. It stands in line. Through studied insistence it supplies the link from precursor to successor—reversing polarity, conductive, sparking. Read, cited, placed. Storied syntagmatic characterization. Comic, tragic. A hero, a scoundrel. Remembered, forgotten. An abandonment. Steady progress. New beginnings. Sovereign capacities. Regression to a mean. Idiosyncratic ways. Sloth, sleuth. Mattering by both paradigmatic assemblance and syntagmatic enchainment.

The noetic knowingly perpetrates institutional crime, practices considered public deceit, pretends something it isn't, dons disguise, and plays the part. The unread passes as that which is. Those in the know are many, willing accomplices. Everyone, so it seems, agrees to how it's done—those seeking standing, security, advancement as well as those deciding the fate of others. Everything by the book. And it, as itself, betrays the pact among co-conspirators regarding its faculties. It signs simply because it is. Unread, cardinal, placed. And being in place determines all. Legion are those who gaze only to confirm the curricular, to catalogue its presence, shelved, hidden in plain sight. And nothing more. Spines fail to crack. Positioning enough, everything. Absence, catastrophic. Misplacement spells tragic displacement, a closing of the book, even upon the most promising. A must-have. A must just-be-seen. A coded prop, a plot-determining coded prop. The unread, a sign in place, determines relations and fates. Mattering simply by presence.

Phenomenology

Fast, furious, to excess—the game at the side. Not in the arena's center, but at its eves. A flurry of madness. Books siding with books. Books pitted against books. Books clamoring about this. Books clamoring about that. Alliances announced, quickly renounced. Speculations abound. Wild speculations. The noetic appears, rises, falls. Book crazy. Book frenzy. Book profusion. So many, hoping so much, realizing so little. Each cherished. Each curated. Each a symbol. Each self-expression. Each an investment. Each presented as if. But each a bet. A side bet. A bet that wagers all on its lines. The book risks all for that which vies one with another: recognition, security, advancement, status, power, *bonus fortuna*. Heavy betting. Eager betting. Too eager. Trusting, too trusting. A wistful demotic hope—all with equal chance—dashed. An invisible feudalism configures divided destinies. Legacy favors the few, the majority suffers, exceptions surprise. Feral aspirations prey to well-policed possibilities. Disappointment exceeded only by disbelief. Semiotics, the mirror held close to sociology. Most consigned to mundanity. Shallow mattering, the endgame of the rigged gamble.

Ineluctable, deliberate, twined—the game in the middle. At center stage. A title match. Those conceived to have their day, destined for the testing of their divinity. In public, for all to see. As it should be. Giants in the ring. Titan leaning against titan. Contestants and contest. Gladiators and game. Banished, the frenzy of the side. Instead, hushed, quiet, all hanging on every word. Banished, too, the asymmetries of the side. Instead, two, equally matched. Doppelgangers. Even money. But this game plays dicey. It is not the sum of all hopes, as at the side, but the sum of fears. Legacy gambling. Ideas cashed as honor. Status—always, only. A status blood bath. Momentous as dangerous. And yet the rules of engagement scrupulously followed. Book nodding to book. A webwork of scripted decorum ensuring respect. The more at stake, the more even the match. But both in over their heads. Such rarity arouses interest, enshrined in memory, woven into lore. Semiotics a mirror. Legacy takes a lifetime. Only a few matter.

Mired in their own significance. And rightly so. A signifier trapped in the web it itself helped spin. Never isolated, always in relation. Each bears meaning, and no two sign the same. Each must thus take up its own meaning and follow it. Such particularity causes gnomic relations to be realized singularly. Sequence and emplacement, the powerful gods of determination. Composed of language they become a language. *Parole* becomes *langue*. They speak volumes.

It is performance. It engages in the assertive, public, cultural ritual of show and tell. The proclaimed can be checked, and double-checked. It is enactment—and triggers re-enactment. It closes that gap between actor and audience by drawing participants into its drama. That it does so depends upon the near religious authority inherent and ascribed. It accepts much, saves much, resolves much. It, a Mass of meaning.

Part III
Writing

§ 6

PARAGRAPH

THE PARAGRAPH THINKS itself a monotheist; but, in truth, a practicing polytheist.

The sentence stars. The spoiled child of writing demands attention and claims credit. Never sated, always moody, the next sits, just out of reach, pouting, refusing to be coaxed. Stubborn as proud, proud as selfish, the single sentence seeks to steal the spot. It, and rarely more, recited, memorized, canonized. Such the sentence's self-indulgence. But when extracted, displaced it struggles to be more than cartouche. Weighty composition hewn of paragraphs—majestic, splendid, complicated paragraphs, aligned and arrayed. Paragraphs, shoulder to shoulder, a phalanx of burden bearing. Paragraph to sentence: sentence to words. The petulant requires the paragraph's discipline. Glory won by sentenced syncopation. The paragraph orders a Morse of sentences, each regulated by semaphore of punctuation. Writing turns on the paragraph—not the sentence. The prodigal sentence enjoys the day only made possible by the paragraph.

The paragraph: the Circus Maximus. Its diegesis of predication, transformation, qualification, coordination, subversion, refutation the forum for veracity, for verisimilitude, for Truth. The paragraph plays host to its own contest. Resolute, the paragraph embarks upon its assigned quest. Its journey one of distinguishing, of testing, of achievement. The paragraph takes up the commission to champion for that which it itself unfolds. The paragraph with a thousand faces. Eloquence—the happy senate of logos, pathos, ethos—lends choreographed aid. Endiku to Gilgamesh. Athena to Telemachus. But dangers lurk at every turn. Clause heaps, profusion piles, indiscriminate as distracting, ever detain, ever threaten. As does the emaciated—thin signifiers lost to powers of de-composition. Concord jeopardized by what's there and what's not. Overdetermined, underdetermined, indeterminate. Writing sends the paragraph into the fray.

A single paragraph—at once, more than less | less than more. Beyond | inside—beyond the fragment, this side of all. A naked paragraph, cordoned by larger and smaller, aggregate and facet, composite and component, ever sentenced to paradigmatic judgments of what's missing. Lonely as liminal, trapped in between. Its properties, proportions, dimensions—each malleable, supple, elastic, and each a mimetic lens to an uncertain semiosis. The mystery of whence mirrors that of whither. Paratextual lack deprives, rendering a paragraph an untethered subject, worded calligraphy, an atemporal metaphor whose only meaningful claim is in-difference. A paragraph, a prescient signifier for plentitude in *absentia*. Such lack, such absence, consigns a solitary paragraph to a singular reliance upon poetics—a dependence that unnerves composure. The writing of a single paragraph ever vexed.

Stochasticity—*a* paragraph's byword. But *the* paragraph never exits in isolation. Παρά-γραφος. Writing beside, composed with. Always adjacent. The paragraph's morphology demands that there be an Other—a second, the second—and the addition of the second transforms *a* into *the*. Indefinite converted to definite through predicate. The first no longer signs as an indeterminant only; the second re-assigns it to a new, paired vocation. The pairing disambiguates the mystery surrounding transmission: the first now reaches for the second, and the second countenances the first. Two, placed together, side by side, defined. The writing of the second presumes the first, and the first finds itself in the second's reflection.

But gains afforded by addition soon mitigated. Two paragraphs, like one alone, manufacture an abundance of lack. Instead of riddles plaguing origins and ends, sender and recipients, whence and whither, a new indeterminacy prevails. The diptych, coupled icons, creates a syntax: the conjoining of two graphical metaphors insists metonymic progression. The two do not simply sit side by side; the first leads to the second. The concatenation of the two—plot's bare minimum—triggers destined teleology. But addition of the second reintroduces ambiguity that begs abduction. The gap between the two creates space that bids imagination to fill. Two paragraphs stare at one another, yearning for yet-to-be-supplied clarification. A missing middle makes the writing of two as provisional as that of one.

The third, the glorious third, makes a threshing floor of the second. The addition of a third paragraph achieves a measure of plentitude. The collocation of the three mimes the full sequence of narrative—a beginning, a middle, an end—and fabricates completed plot. The addition of the third supplies the missing middle, a middle that was already hidden in plain sight in the second. All that was needed to reveal the second as middle was the addition of the third. The middle was there all along. The third clarifies what prompts (the first), prompting's ends (the third) and what conveys the first to third (the second). The addition of the third changes the second from recipient of the first's transmission to that which ferries the first to the third. The third alters the role of the second—and thus its nature. The second regathers, re-composes. In the writing of the third the second learns to play the verb between two nouns.

The third potentiates that which will not find conclusion until the final paragraph. The third's valency makes paradigm of the second, urging it to exemplify that which characterizes all paragraphs that intervene: every preceding paragraph, by intent or serendipity, falls under the spell of the one that follows. Such the curious powers of enchainment. Each paragraph cascades, crashing into the next, while the next reframes the previous. Metonymy and boustrophedon, simultaneous, by accretion.

The placement of the next reveals the liminality of the previous. Every intervening paragraph occupies the boundary that divides the sequence. All paragraphs that intervene become a side street, a hallway, a lobby. All are hypnagogic. They dare affiliation. On the move, always navigating, never at home. All are transgressive. Every intervening paragraph thus lycanthropic: compositional forces change what precedes when caught in the beams of what follows. With any addition the previous alters. Liminality and lycanthropy by accretion.

Self-contained yet related, organic yet constructed, complete yet lacking, a cessation yet swirling, singular yet multiple, pragmatic yet arbitrary, arabesque yet periodic, cadenced yet staccato, essence yet chimera, *mythos* yet *dianoia*, metaphor yet metonymy—the paragraph riddles writing even as it figures writing. Above and beyond the happenstance and the careless, the paragraph composes fraternal order. The addition of its Other—and other's Other—seeks the harmony won only by the knowing ability to play the subject, the verb, and the object at moment's notice. The paragraph does many things by being many things. The paragraph, never just a one.

§ 7

VOICE

Sozzled voice dreams a starry night of many readers. Somber voice knows what it knows—there's but one audience.

Voice, imagined as *aide de champ*, protégé, flag. Voice, conceived ever present help. Expectations high. Demands great. Voice—a golden lamp, sword from stone, magic dust. Voice, presumed Mentor, guide, accomplice.

Voice pressed into contrived service. Young voice, pliable voice, impressionable voice, eager-to-please voice. Need and invention conscript. Voice, the suborned opportunist, the reluctant chameleon. Asked to reach these, reach those. To reach here, there. To reach any, some, most, all. Voice, messianic panacea. Voice, consuetude. But voice bedridden, exhausted, frazzled, unable to fit the bill. Aspirations, lofty aspirations. Voice's shoulders prove too narrow. Voice tasked with the impossible. Voice powerless to find, forgive, fix bookish sin. Curry does that—and more. But not voice. Voice's destined virtuosity realized elsewhere.

The allure of readers tempts. Their specter entices, chance beguiles, magic strong. To succumb defensible, understandable. Votives to readers sold cheap at every stand—and advice for finding offered at every corner. So easy to buy, hope. So easy to exchange the birthright of audience for a readers' pot of porridge.

The personal—the I, the we—a Turkish Delight that deceives the noetic with assurances of vast acclaim. The I, alleged charm that makes friends of strangers. The I does answer a call. The I of the margins, the I of the excluded, the I of the oppressed, the I of the forgotten. That I makes visible, disrupts, dislodges, contests. That I mandated. That I insists imagination. That I tears down, builds new. That I effective. That I marries prayers to preaching, and preaching to practice. Also the I of legacy. The I of surrender and ardor. Not the I of garrulous personality, but of the humbled wisdom. That I commands attention. That I earned. That I trusted. That I needed.

Voice's I exceptions—the disinherited, the sage. Otherwise, the first singular works the opposite of hoped. The personal voice forces the book to teeter atop too tiny a fulcrum. The whole of the book's what turns upon an indeterminate who—a ghost, a thin and disguised persona, one without past or papers. The I raises questions, spawns suspicion. I fails to foster the trust it seeks. The plural first no better, maybe worse. We entails I's deficiency, but also it counterfeits community, simulates concern, supposes yet to be established relations. Presumptuous we. If the first estranges and pretends, direct address still more brazen. If the personal invites, the vocative intrudes. It barges in, bellows, breaking tranquility. Suspension demolished—no going back. The first, in all its forms, courts woe.

Original sin conflates readers and audience, as if the garden has but one tree. But two trees grow there, and both bestow fruit. Voice reveals the self-deception of conceiving the two as one. The book may be *for* readers, but it's *to* an audience. And voice divulges the book itself as the only audience it has—or will ever have. The book writes to itself, not to readers. Conceit imagines readers on, and for, every page. Voice reveals the book devoid of the authority, the powers, the ability to create an audience outside itself. Voice exposes the book's limitation. Voice shows that a book cannot gather to one place, at one time, a collective, for a shared experience of reading. Voice fails the task assigned to it. Readers, a penurious synonym for audience.

The concert, the contest, the theater, the lecture. The rally, the race, the game, the play, the dance. Performers create, and the created performance unique—like the sunrise, the summer day, the thunderstorm. The unrepeatable moment. Experienced just once—but a once with a with. Performance lives between, between those performing and those experiencing. Performance binds the two. The drama inherent to performance draws. Performance draws those who experience the performance closer to the performance itself—and to each other. Performance baptizes the collective into a one. All that differentiates those that gather in one place, at one time, for one purpose, held at bay, bracketed, suspended, by the power of experience. Performance stops time. Performance dissolves diversity. Performance births audience. The collective response—jubilation, adulation, celebration, appreciation, awe, disappointment, sorrow—a choral commentary upon the power of performance to create one of many. Eleusis' mysteries still at work.

Readers are not so. Readers do not constitute audience. Glorious, persnickety, fussy readers. Readers read in isolation, at their own pace, and in their own way. At desk, in bed, on beach. Read fast, slow, fast again. Put down; pick up. Skip around, skip over. Re-read, read backwards. Readers read as readers wish. Listless as avid. Readers follow no rule, heed no advice. Nothing governs reading, and nothing about the habits of readers mirrors the conventions of audience. The sum of all readers may comprise market, but not audience. The stray, the isolated, the sequestered never a communal one. Pure fiction to think otherwise. Readers as fragmented and fickle as reading is idiosyncratic and iterative. The book faces readers just once, and then only to pre-face. The story behind, story of. Twists, turns, trials, trails. The book's own memoir—how, against odds. The author's own story—how, against odds. No book originates apart from the sacrifice of self. The weaving of the two well suited.

But once the first note sounds, once the curtain rises, once the page turns, the book takes over, and voice inflects anew. Gone preamble's self-obsessive apologia. Voice announces the book's performance, endowed with the power to create its own audience. Itself. Narrative performs. The book renders service to itself—and only itself—an encounter that constitutes voice. This encounter dangerous enough. To face, and not merely pre-face, the inner demonic exposes the talk of readers as trivial. To employ voice to aim at readers too shallow, too crass, too vulgar. Voice aimed at readers renders the book vacillating, frivolous. Authors who speak to readers murder the narrator. But voice's true destiny, its performance, truly a matter of life and death. Voice descends. Persephone rescued.

Four elements. Four winds. Four voices. The four comprise the book's realm: the compelling, the invisible, the judicious, the prophetic. The realm knows peace when the discernable four win happy consonance.

To begin daunting. The endeavor acknowledged challenge. The blank paralyzes. Voice seeks to master empty chaos. Words into the void. Tentative, unsure, pre-mature. The blank terrifies. So easy to shrink. Real daring to get it write. Voice quick to surrender to the mechanical's tug; the Muse scurries off. Voice plays it safe. The result confusing, if predictable. Mimicry instead of magic. Formula instead of Faerie. A voice jumble—the wearisome rehearsal of who said what when; the tedious account of the

Voice

borrowed, better how; the mollycoddled recital of everything to come; all lumped with the indulgent, pitched in the halting or trumpeted bluster—a voice mishmash. Nuts and bolts and crackers and pennies. To commence defaults to ad hoc: the menagerie of what's left over, the patchwork of the misfitted and misplaced. Adventure falls prey to the preliminary.

To name the what, to define that what by comparison with the near, the distant, the diametric, to delimit what's scope—yes. To furnish the essential, warn of mires, and detours, and goblins—yes again. All assistive, but all equally insufficient. Voice must realize what's required to start. Beginning's voice announces the book's impending journey. Voice is not the journey nor even the journey's itinerary, but the journey's prompt. Voice the journey's why. Voice the journey's obsession. Voice sends, commissions. To start gives voice to desire, and voice desires book's end. Voice gazes through the book, reaches for its end, yearning for its plentitude. So pressing voice's obsession for book's end that it compels. No going back. The journey inevitable. Initial voice insists it so. Commissioning's voice direct, judicious, circumspect while playing the affective and psychological provocateur. The book's realization of voice's commission in the book's prose another matter. But the voice of the start burdens, intrigues, insists, propels, involves without wasting or wanting. The weightiest of matters arise from the most tidy beginnings.

To turn the page is to change the voice. The imperative ebbs, the authoritative flows. Voice begins a new chapter. The invisible takes the stage to star between beginning and end. That voice never calls attention to itself. That voice embodies the personal by avoiding notice. That voice out of sight but never absent—and never devoid of influence. That voice dependent upon anonymity. That voice authoritative, trusted, cognitive. That voice works texture. That voice builds density. That voice gives depth. That voice puts the book's prose in the front row to experience its many descriptions, interpretations, analyses, syntheses, extrapolations. That voice knows the book is not the subject of the book. That voice refuses the temptation to quote *iterum atque iterum et in extensio*. Flaccid surrogates may salve the insecure but never lend tenor to voice. That voice does not twaddle off into public debates over the history of elves. Muse bids prose voice to address the only audience the book enjoys—itself.

Notes argue the history of elves to the letter—their existence, size, shape, age, number, composition, habits, history, provenance, names, language, texts, ways, influence. Notes debate how to study elves, quantitatively, qualitatively, and regale the storied ins and outs of elvish *Forschungsgeschichte*. Notes consider the implications of elves—economic, social, political, racial, gender. Notes render a verdict on every elvish issue of elvish consequence. Notes open every elvish door to elvish every room and looks in every elvish box. Notes never complacent nor neglectful when it comes to elves. Elves matter, and whatever elvish matters. Notes never confuse elves with humans or hobbits.

Notes, the beneficiary of voice's inflectional enchantments: directional, pointing to prose's acts of dependance and sources of authority; informative, arming prose with the studied; evaluative, weighing evidence and conclusions about evidence; defensive, mounting responses for proffered judgments; perspectival, placing evidence and its claims in context; conjectural, daring to speculate about the peripheral; conversational, fostering sustained dialogue with consociates. Voice steady, intrepid, technical, comprehensive, masterful. Voice terse, impatient, nettlesome, cranky, opinionated. Voice allows notes to make possible prose's journey.

To conclude awakens the cultural prophet from its long bookish slumber. What has been insisted, realized, fortified now speaks a word, a word in pursuit of that which is without remainder. The voice of the end refuses the safe harbor of summary. Content to recount is to flinch, hide, shrink. Final voice summons courage to dare the needed bold. That voice dreams risk, countenances sacrifice—its own blood inked into hope's every line. To finish never full stop. Closure opens to Justice, longs for reversal of wrong's many cold sentences. But prophetic voice tethered, careful to connect ends with means. Voice crafts end to beginning's desire and middle's substance. Ethos married to logos and pathos. Voice realizes as visible that long held invisible. Voice's many words become a word—even the Word.

Four elements. Four winds. Four voices. Each discreet. Each potent. Yet, when four find society, the book enjoys concord. A four-for-all of voice. The four a blessed trinity.

Voice appears only when all prayers rightly uttered and all rightly sacrificed. Voice made and makes. Voice begotten and begets. Voice remembers, remembered. Voice discontented, full. Voice searches, discovered. Voice momentary, lasting. Voice, a fickle quarto, anchored unity. Voice, the conjured and enchanter. Voice refuses authorial narcissism, preferring its textual own. Readers, voice's mortal enemy. Audience, voice's only aid. Voice not a how, but a what, a what of desire. Voice, object of book's desire. Book, object of voice's desire. Voice results when the book discovers itself. The book results when voice discovers itself. Vocal reciprocity rules the bookish realm.

§ 8

PLOT

IDEAS ARE PEOPLE too. Ideas surprise—or should. Ideas slay dragons. Ideas solve mysteries. Ideas host their own Bacchanalia. Ideas paint, sing, dance. Ideas travel, discover, map. Ideas disrupt, tear down, re-make. Ideas somaticize, give, sacrifice. Ideas follow the stars. Ideas live as if they have something to prove, to leave an indelible mark. Ideas live for tomorrow—and as if there's no tomorrow. Ideas long for the unimaginable. Ideas come of age to venture the unexpected. Ideas tiresome when tame. Ideas whose ends entailed in their beginning bore. Ideas excite when prodigal. Wild, uncontrollable, feral. Ideas, even the most noetic, yearn for the far country. Best they go where they will, then followed.

Ideas often booby-trapped before their endeavors begin. Discovery's what, mechanics, gears, and claims stifle telling's inventions. The unknown, unexplained, misunderstood—subject's relics so rare, so potent, that the relic itself dictates narration. The cunning, crafty, clever—discovery so ingenious that narration forced to retrace its steps. The new, totalizing, explosive—method so explanatory that narration held hostage to the procedural. The mathematical, measured, inevitable—argument so conclusive that narration bows to ordered propositions. The book made prey, surrendering narration's glory to the whims of subject, fortunes of research, potency of tools, or coldness of logics. Epistemology, narratology's younger sibling, supplants. But heuristics prove a poor second. Narration, a protagonist of gravity, transcends discovery.

Design chases invention, narration follows ideas. Ideas suggest their own telling. Ideas evoke their own recital. Ideas whisper their own arrangement. Ideas insinuate their own bind. But invention's cues haphazard, incomplete, allusive at best. Young ideas, self-obsessed, leave design to fend for itself. Paralysis, the result of early writing's ambiguities. First writing incomplete. Erratic, moody, messy. First writing unresponsive, recalcitrant. First writing craves discipline, yet stiffens its neck. Starting, stumbling, stopping. Sentences jumbled, mounded, idea fragments raked into graphical piles. Coherence slippery, configuration mercurial, plot fleeting.

Patience, resolve, tolerance. Mercy, fortitude, impartiality. Ruthlessness. The willingness to abandon, change course. Nothing inked scriptural, deemed canonical, until composition's end. All up for grabs. Tentative, provisional, exploratory. But miracle *in medias res*. Water from wine, order out of chaos. The concatenation of the ill-shaped suggests the outlines of patterned arc. Epiphany grants sightline. The travails of first writing slowly—painfully—births plot. Plot conceived by idea's arrangement. Plot organizes ideas as Marduk the constellations. Never imposed, always organic. Plot dares to govern narration's arc as sympathetic, benevolent monarch. Plot steers narration between Sisyphus and Tiamat, between relics and reckless, between cold logic and wild.

Plot, surfaced and named, off to work. Plot, the syntax of and for ideas. Plot orders, arranges, satisfies. Plot—like genre—never pristine. Permutations abound. But plot—like genre—coalesces,

Plot

aggregates, thickens. Plot's singular shape emerges, recognizable, despite writing's muddle.

Action. The struggle between good and evil, right and wrong. Narration structured by enemy's vanquish. Pure proairesis, noetic bread and butter. Emplotment follows the discernable. The description of what's amiss—what ideational depravation, what absence, what suppression, what invisibility. The identification of what malevolent, ideational power dare disturb—and analysis of why. The prophetic prognosis of what ideational catastrophe exists, looms. The anointing of what ideational power rights the wrong and the interpretive commentary of how. The roll call of ideational help, and the lettered inditement of that which doesn't. The denouement. The moment ideas' struggle against ideas held in balance. Graphic telling of tables turned before celebration of the futures made possible by ideational success. Variability of proportion, predictability in arrangement.

Abduction. The struggle between mystery and perspicuity, true and false. Narration structured by enigma's explanation. Pure hermeneutics, noetic bread and butter. Emplotment follows the discernable. Diegesis begins after—after the telling of so singular a tale, so inexplicable, so garbled, that the nonsensical reigns. Bewilderment. The mazed rules. No existing postulation suffices. The sifting of how the previously proffered fails to account for disparity only further confounds. The easy, the glib, insufficient forms the suspenseful foil for narration's deferment of final, full resolution. Abduction embraces the improbable, the seeming impossible. Abduction works back. Abduction derived from the small, suggested by the unobserved and ignored, discovered by attending to the gaps and erasures. Abduction rooted and grounded in the trivial, the bothersome, unaccounted. But such abduction spurned as reckless conjecture, dogged as mere guesswork. Abduction, without apology, affirms the consequent.

Abduction refuses the partial to dare an explanatory, enchained, singular whole. Abduction's risk rewarded. Abduction's revelation then tested. Resolution confirmed by the re-telling that renders a full accounting. Variability in proportion, totalizing in final disposition.

Iconic. The struggle between diffusive and ruled, oscillated and orchestrated. Narration comprised by arabesque. Pure eros, noetic bread and butter. Emplotment follows the discernable. Temporality, essential to action and abduction, surrenders to the suspended, the dilatory. Description. Description piled. Description stacked. Description stacked high. Thick description stacked high. Prodigious, self-indulgent, thick description stacked high and tall. Patient, prodigious, self-indulgent thick description stacked high and tall. Patient, prodigious, self-indulgent thick description dripping with color, depth, and resonance stacked high and tall. Details relished. Details revered. Details worshiped. Precision, nuance, granularity. Chapter and verse. Copious, exhaustive, profuse. Unapologetic. Ornate, baroque, plethoric. The glory of what's there. Compounded. Amplified. Lavish scene. Lavish seen. Truth in description. Truth through description. Variability of proportion, convincing in visuality.

Cartographic. The struggle between order and disorder, *victi mundi* and *terra nullis*. Narration constituted by taxonomic symmetry. Mapping, noetic bread and butter. Emplotment follows the discernable. Ideational phylum named. Borders drawn. The pertinent framed. Edged delimitation critical to utility. Filters and scaling applied. Conceptual arrangements trade in graphic exclusion, distortion, imposition. Maps leave out. Maps fictive. Maps substitute. Exclusion and figural distortion key to charting representational relationships, and the cartographer's symbolling an inevitable cultural imposition. Legends—credits, names, dates, sources histories, influences—coded shorthand, embedded

Plot

locators. The world of ideas lost without maps. The world of ideas with inaccurate maps oppressive. Good maps draw judicious lines. Good maps orient. Good maps honest. Ideational cartography ages. The world of ideas, once ordered, changes. The factual destined to become artifactual, as new lines drawn. Variability in rendering, reliability in positioning.

 Episodic. The tension between autonomous and enmeshed, insular and entwined. Narration comprised by serialization. Pure juxtaposition, noetic bread and butter. Emplotment follows the discernable. The periodic compilation of the discreet. Chapters subsist in themselves. Each a standalone. Each self-reliant. Each adheres to pattern. Each delivers the analogous. Each exemplifying the whole *in nuce*. The succession of the similar beaded together. Links between, among the parts tenuous. Ideas alone bind. Desire for ordered concatenation rendered inconsequential. Episodes metaphoric rather than metonymic—calligraphy chosen over epic—ever risking replication. While one episode inconclusive, periodic's sum achieves desired ends. Little variability in telling, insistence through aggregation.

 Ideas breathe life into plot. Without ideas, plot a lifeless form. As a good book reminds, ideas were not made for plot, but plot for ideas. Ideas over the fence.

§ 9

CONTENTS

A LIST. MUNDANE, pedestrian, tedious. Left to itself a table regresses to the analogical, the finite. Table's nature seeks the cataloging of all. The forgivable result of sustained wrestling with the innumerable, a table attempts to tame chaos. Table as index. Table as mere contents.

Judged by wholeness, by completeness, by a calculated, measured mathematical precision. Wedding participants. The receipt at the end of dinner. The number of forks in the drawer, shoes in the closet, acres of land. Contents as census. Contents as balance sheet. Contents as outline. Honest, straightforward, perfectly analogous. Dull. Dull as accurate.

All true, but not all truth.

Overtelling bores. Obsessive naming banishes all mystery. Profusion of detail saps all fantasy dry. Exacting correspondence murders the hope of impossibility. Contents discontented. But, a part, and not the whole—indeed, a part in place of the whole. Concision, the smell of Athena's sweet ambrosia. Encoded, a table's sacrificial offering to the gods.

A table poetry, not facsimile. A table story, not reproduction. A table whispers about what's long been hidden, mysterious causes, lasting effects. A table cautiously retraces history's erasures. A table makes harmony and symmetry out of disparate and disproportioned. Not fit, but match. A table maps the *terra incognito*, a world discovered soon to be visited by many others.

A table arcs. Invokes, invites, anticipates. A table bends. It imagines plot's rise, horizon to horizon. A table launches the voyager. It awakens from slumber, shaking sleep from the eyes. It pushes toward the journey ahead. A table excites, tantalizes, tempts. A table full of possibilities, of promises made and to be kept.

A table one—but not one to one. A table never wooden. A table is never content masquerading as an index. A table heralds even as it creates. A table lives between Calypso's tempting memory and Penelope's warm embrace. There, and only there, does the table enjoy true contentment.

Part IV
Writers

§ 10

SOCIOLOGY

The what of writing exegesis—commentary upon what's who, who's where, where's how.
    The fortunes of what and who enlace. What seeks audience—who enjoys readers. What dreams of triumph—who bears rejection. What parades who for all to see. Who conceives what as objective product only to discover that what insists who be subjective partner. What, even the most noetic what, acts upon who. Who creates what; but what shapes who. What's inscribed *telos* transforms who's *ontos*.
    What reveals who's where. Unseen forces informing who's circumstances dictate what and how to who. What and how arrive preset. Write as has already been written. Conventions drilled. Learned, practiced, re-drilled. Ritual incantation, social recitation. What apes that upon which it depends. What's thousand years of tradition oversees who's apprenticeship. The compact of noetic reproduction underwrites craft and guild. Context forges capacities. Context impresses praxis. Context scripts text. What dons where's uniform. Who's what ruled by where's compositional orthodoxy. Adherence earns acceptance. Compliance gains admittance. Proficiency wins acclaim.

The scientific birthed the noetic how. *Societas*—itself the genetic progeny of the scientific—how's appointed *paidagogos*. Once composed, how serialized as noetic *lingua franca*. *Universitas* anointed the scientific how as the grammar for its language. Apprenticeship's final test, gateway to *collegium*, is the scientific how writ large. The most sacred of noetic of promises judged by the scientific how—and how much. The scientific how, noetic coin of the realm.

Not every noetic writes a book. Nor should they. The serial the most flawless and economic means of conveyance for scientific discovery. Scope defined, circumscribed. Data fresh, newly generated, time sensitive. Method experimental, self-conscious. The demands of predictability make repetition a must. Results incremental, analytical, pragmatic. Form, as ubiquitous as monotonous, resplendently apt.

Books are not so. No two the same. Singularity in rendering mirrors compositional invention and subject peculiarity. Sources—venerable, lavishly curated, well-rehearsed. The accidents of history and the politics of preservation make repetition impossible. Results totalizing, abductive, existential. Narrative, ambitious yet riddled by constant deferral, resplendently apt. The two rule their respective noetic realms, each sovereign in their domain.

The noetic embrace, practice, reprisal of the scientific how's power reveals it bully to the humanist aspirations. The scientific how's impositions never go unnoted. Repeated adherence to its established way begins a slow decline. Individuality withers in the face of conformity's power. Mimesis, devoid of improvisation, steals. To diverge toys with risk and potential shunning. Far safer to subscribe the scientific how's restrictive canonical covenants. The gods have said it must be so. Univocal, detached, sterile. No artistry, no invention. Sources, method, and argument vie for prominence, banishing voice and story. The poet wanes.

Sociology

To write in a way different than imposed proves daunting. The need to conform wages holy war. Who, what, how—beholden to where. Precision grapples with the poetic, method with artistry, and repeatability with singularity. The physics of the measured true—the observable, quantifiable, predictable—differ in phylum, genus, and species from the hermeneutics of the romantic Truth—the ontological, the eternal, the ineffable. Poets measure by a different star, as stories—not atoms—comprise their universe.

§ 11

SOCIAL PSYCHOLOGY

THE TOLL BEGS why. Time, imagination, fortitude. Nothing easy. Endless, discouraging, perfunctory. Distracted, bored, stuck. Guilt-ridden, fearful, uninspired. Alone.

The grind leads to something else—primary means to particular end. Finishing. Reason enough. No one suffers out of its love. But none reach journey's end without it. And lots of it. Demanded, what's composed the measuring stick. But never reduced to means without remainder. Resilient, it lives on with a mind of its own. Wicked, unpredictable, surprising. Something prompts, something unmanageable, something wild and unruly. Something refusing suppression. Something anonymous. A drive, a desire, a dream. What arises from the depths enables survival.

Compulsive, even when commodified. Ideas committed to page mirror composer. The pressured stirs within, awakening dormant joys or unwelcome disclosures. Confidence, recognition, pride. Or dread, pure dread. The act betrays the forces swirling beneath. But that which threatens to reveal too much proves therapeutic: ordered lines lend sentenced help. The page calms, assures, in-forms. Taming private chaos never complete, even if composition establishes the curious marriage of compliance with art, objective with subjective, detached with expressive.

Obligation, obsession—the opening chapters. Anxiety follows. Out of and into. Prospects of securing, and then remaining, ever haunt. Lettering at every turn. Compliance debases zeal to stress, desire to duress.

Completion's euphoria fades, the metric for noetic standing sinks in. Only the printed bequeaths recognition, identifies as on the way up, with ideas, a future, to watch, to know, destined. Only the printed garners the most senior's attention—and its signatory secreted for this and that. Only the printed makes badge's name memorable. Not just any will do. Heft, gravity, depth, breadth. Gauntlet's survivor must be graced by a colophon of renown. To be assayed, cited, recited, required. Expectations high. Anxiety reigns.

No schooling for such new imposition—and how inhibited. Time, energy confiscated—preps, students, pedagogy, students, meetings, accountability, assessment, community, students—black holes and landmines. Powers huff and puff. Stray invitations—accepted, regretted. The successes of others stoke fires of jealousy, guilt, and self-loathing. Jealousy, guilt, self-loathing, and fear. A zero-sum game afoot. Hopelessness as circular as democratic.

The unrevised receives backing from all who care. Problem solved, pressure relieved—so it seems. The dedicated exists, but for scarce number and chosen few. The unrevised's double duty stresses its fabrication beyond fracture. Genre a despot, rendering verdict without mercy. Sobering truth: the unrevised is the unrevised and nothing more. Period. That precious few fancy the unrevised compels revision. Revising, the only labor more hellish than the rote. No preparation, no seminar, no academy, no roadmap, no guide. No model, or exemplar, or point of reference. Only the awareness that what's bound now binds.

Social Psychology

Learning the quad's labyrinth begins early. But nothing prepares for the byzantine. A dizzying array confronts. To which, what differentiates among, do differences matter? When, how, what? All, some, none? Admit, hide? Wait or press? More than one? When to concede? What then? Only broken links between the newly minted, burdened by the unrevised, and those who possess fated power. Improbability staggers the novice. And yet the first must be.

The calculated practice of exclusion reduces, if not robs, of opportunity. Language and genre—monitored, guarded. Sources and methods—monitored, guarded. Access and means—monitored, guarded. Apprenticeship, wearing thin disguise, keeps in line. The first, so it seems, must conform. Voice discounted, tamed, quieted. Voice made to speak an-other's language. But voice finds a way. Discontented, Voice takes the stage. Voice delivers new lines, follows new script, spurns old direction. Voice defies being made invisible. Voice contests all that guards. Voice breaks up, tears down. Voice corrects. Voice includes. Voice builds fresh. Voice makes new beginnings as a first. Mattering by difference.

Once forgivable, twice aggrievement. The second a ticket, transaction, exchange. No glory. Such the oblation. The second proves the first no fluke, if only to its consignor. Find, marshal, produce. Technical, narrow—just more. More of the mechanical, more of the obligatory, more ritual. Love-hate sours to hate-hate. Resentment simmers. Credentialed, accepted, secure—collapse. Two squeezed from one renders anything, everything else alluring. The self that sought solace in lettered lines finds enchantments in well-practiced paideutics or governing's dark arts. The compulsive self, the obligatory self, the anxious self takes leave, wandering off to a far country. The creative fancies the prodigal. Realities soon whistle back such recklessness.

Vouchsafed, secure—corner turned. Dreams, long dormant, flower. Vitality, freedom, confidence replace survival, anxiety, obligation. Ideas, in abundance, daily dance in and out. They beckon, they charge, they insist. *Vocatio*. The empty fills. Prospects no longer suffer. Once daunting, even hopeless, now natural, even automatic. Opportunities multiply. Polarities reverse: interest, bids, respect. From scarcity and panic to abundance and calm. A new who.

Call toys with form. Stifling generic prescriptions lift. The demands of the technical, with its inward coil, confine no longer. Vocation follows the outward spiral. Vocation leverages convention to release what's locked inside. Structure no longer beholden to guilded impositions. Vocation traces a different arc. Vocation matches tool to task. Ideas cease serving genre, and genre now bows to ideas. Proving tucked inside telling. A new how.

Temptation regresses to the mean of those whose legitimation first sought. But the vocational resists. The vocational gives voice to calling through alignment. In vocation, the what, and the why what matters keep house. Who's temperament, habits, virtues find concord in the what and the how—and with the few equally called to steward. Ideas, rooted, trigger other bonds. Congruence opens to discovery of integral ties with larger publics. Vocation prizes inclusion, and an improbable number find their way to the table forged by vocation's lettered expression. This inner ring, made possible by call, reveals that guild does not own all. The vocational belongs to the community it itself forges. Vocation proves that ideas do matter—and for many.

Vocation creates a series of the composed. A random but broken line emerges. The enchainment tells a story—be it intentional or by serendipity. The accumulation desires its own plentitude. Perceived lack prioritizes, motivating the search for completion. Vocation weighs the odds of achievement against time. Focused, determined. Looking forward to what remains in an imperceptible instant gives way to looking back to order what is. Story gives way to sense-making. *Mythos* to *dianoia*. Vocation pillows its head only to awake as legacy.

Legacy takes stock. Legacy distills. Legacy indexes. Legacy stewards. Legacy bequeaths. Obligation returns—but legacy's obligation born of humility, not of hubris or approval. Vocation's totality imposes the burden. Gift compels responsibility. Legacy shoulders the full weight of duty. Legacy transcends.

Legacy takes varied forms. Legacy yearns to gather into a whole. The compendium produces a new figure through the very act of assemblage. Legacy finds expression in the essential. Only the well-traveled knows what's needed, what should go into the case—and what can and should be left behind. Legacy also seeks remembrance. The intellectual, the personal provides commentary on the external. Hidden influences—ideas, experiences, mentors—indirect parables. But nothing more legacy than big.

Big can come early, even first. But curse as much as blessing if it does. Early and big brings hard reckoning: not every is or can be. The bar once set makes again nightmarish preoccupation. But fear to perform twice exceeded only by terror in doing it once. The vocational faces the inevitable big examination. Questions whispered at cocktails parties and committees alike. No *vitae* considered fully *curriculum* without *magnum*.

Big, no mere skirmish. Big, an all-out campaign. Vocation resolves scuffles; legacy revolution. Vocation, tactical; legacy, strategic. Big tackles big. Big faces that which matters most. Big, not every box every room. Big discerns—every box that matters and only boxes that do. Big never shrinks, no matter the difficulty. Big never wastes. Big lives by parsimony. Big and apt. Big never content with small. But big refuses to overwrite importance with size. Big bored by fiddling. Big solves crimes. Big sees big. Big explains big.

Big changes the game. Big dares to be wrong—and not by a little. Big risks big. Big's heuristics soar as its certainty plummets. Big and ironic. Only big punctuates.

Why persists. Why lingers. Why at every stage. Why, who's Muse. Nothing easy. All hard won. Nothing pointless. Obsession, obligation, anxiety transfigured as vocation, stewardship. Why lives many lives. Why ceases to be chore when aligned.

Why's tipping point. Wind. Water. Fire. Earth. Primal. Artistry's alchemy. Such why anchors a day, a week, a month, a soul, a life. Such is its own why.

Part V
Publishing

§ 12

EDITORS

BOOKS, INCARNATIONS. WRITING, living. Publishers, servants. Editors, shamans.

Arrogant, fickle, sympathetic. Passionate, mysterious, unpredictable. Feared, hated, loved. Affable, encouraging, dismissive. Restless, inscrutable, enthusiastic. Hungry, hard, supportive. Bold, visionary, skeptical. Perpetually curious, easily bored. Riddled by no, graced with yes.

Editors wake desperate—for the new, old, hidden, forgotten, wise. Editors listen. Editors question, imagine, extrapolate, connect. Editors peer deep inside—conjuring, incanting, naming. Editors recklessly wager all on a single roll. Editors mentor, freely sharing all they know. Editors counsel, advise, helping paper and ink become vocation. Editors hide, playing hard to get, to take desire's full measure. Editors set unachievable standards— and callously demand compliance. Editors motivate, encourage, comfort. Editors present during darkest moments of despair. Editors do not flinch to speak truth, however hard.

Hunters, coaches, therapists, friends, colleagues, experts, magicians, carny barkers, technicians, advocates, partners, judges, gate keepers, poets, priests, prophets, pirates. At their best, midwives, stewards, champions, sponsors. At their worst, capricious, foolish, self-absorbed, stubborn, wasteful. Sworn at, sworn by. Enigmas. Contradictions. A sunny spring day, a bitter winter storm. Poem and nightmare enlaced. Editors empower and thwart in equal measure. Editors whisk across the dance floor, while demanding stepped perfection.

Editors—real editors, good editors, true editors—bail the water alongside. Bucket after bucket. Their survival, their life, inextricably knotted to that of those they serve. Two fates bound together by a single book.

§ 13

PRESSES

PRESSES BEFUDDLE. PRESSES befuddle as publishing bewilders. Anonymous, esoteric, fantastical. Magic behind a veil— hidden, protected. The transubstantiation of words to Word never explained. To do so profanes the mystery. To do so reduces ancient art to simple math. To do so disappoints desire: those who risk their all in lettered lines crave the sorcery, the conjuring, the holy rites. Only the wonderous suffices. Only wizardry satisfies. Only alchemy will do. Blood begs the smoke.

Mysteries performed in secret publicly mirrored in quixotic plumage. Pavilioned, draped, bannered. The entirety compressed into the calculated politic. Intense, distilled, intentional. Tables tell all. Press next to press. Tables turned. Press vying with press. The clash of heraldic colors signals epic joust. *Cote de arms*, a sign. Spectacle, a language. Symbolic, iconic, storied. But no translator for the novice or the versed. All consigned to their own invention—to interpret difference and devise waypoint. Few clues. Noetic bewilderment forgivable.

Prestige, plunder, purpose. Now abide these three. But the greatest of these their sum. All seek all. Prestige universal ambition. Plunder universal benchmark. Purpose universal mission. All sound alike, all look alike. But each mixes in different measure. Each composure unique. No two identical. Similar, but distinct. Sometimes ever so slight. But small scales large. Appearances deceive. They lull, cloud, impair. What can make or break obscured by resemblance. Noetic frustration understandable.

Fingerprinting reveals singularity. Size often, but not always, capacity's visible predictor of virtuosity in all registers—noetic, transformative, affective. Footprints range from near neighborhood to that which spans. Less observable the valences of ownership, even when designated. Partisan roots cloaked in noetic neutrality. Antiquity confers a blessing all its own. Those of more recent origins left to proffer fresh air. Scope conveys wisdom and prowess—or betrays foolish conceit. Selectivity, the touted premium of exceptionalism. But such exclusivity, perchance, renders insular, smacks provincial and smug. Underwriting adequate, even considerable, offered willingly and in total, exchanged for the privilege to steward, save for those that cajole in kind or gouge sums. Pecuniary, as ever, the root of all difference. Shaping, crafting, wording—time, time lavished and lacquered for the good. Or, buying, selling, pushing—commodity, simply goods in abundance. The quiet atelier or the fuss of brokerage. Assembled, mechanical, an object. Bespoke, crafted, a subject. Disposable or durable. Momentary or gnomic. Differences cultured and appraised in discrete figurations.

Prestige. All glorious prestige—legacies savor it, monikers seek it. For a handful, one word enough. More than enough. The one word tells all. Name near sacred. Ancient, aristocratic, affluent. Cardinal, powerful, expansive. A juggernaut, a leviathan. Discriminating, exclusive, inscrutable. Assured, calm, composed. Renown by parentage, prospered by inheritance. Affordances paid back—pressed down, shaken together, overflowing. Equals equally ancient, accordingly haute. Sought for the rarity of what's long been banked—but never shown, shared, sold. Pursuit of such goods leads to purgatory—to wait, an eternity. The decision, a crucible. Junior and senior alike weak-kneed at first hint of news. Imbalance obvious, as individuated gravity dwarfed by sponsor's fame. Rented prestige. Exclusion reigns as the handful admits only a handful. The club kept small. Legacy's prestige salted by meritocracy's promise.

For others, legacy's close kin, it's the nominal suffix that counts—not its prefix. Accent falls upon syntax's last two members—not the weighty first. The one words trade on clubby heritage. Their cousins simply by belonging to the family. The former raises noetic eyebrows; the latter checks a noetic box. But no gainsaying. Monikers approved, tested, trusted. Dedicated, focused, assistive. Their endeavors noetic bread and butter. Responsible, essential, foundational. There to confirm, to warrant, to credential. Monikers perform the assigned, the needed. And well. But not all equal. Perceived proximity to what legacies horde determines perceived rank. Nothing left to do but covet what can never be obtained—and then bicker over vanity's unwanted cloak. Moniker's prestige diminished by meritocracy's illusion.

Plunder. All glorious plunder. All seek it. All want it. All need it. All measure by it. Yet few admit its centricity. Most hem and haw. Hard to come clean about avarice. An impolite truth too gauche for public accounting. Too pedestrian, too base, too ambitious, too calculated. For some, truly but a tool. But for others, the only goal. For some, the means to impact. For others, what matters most.

Plunder's pursuit by factory or fame. Factory indiscriminate, fame selective. Factory insentient, anonymous. Fame, each a star. Factory scales to volume. Fame grooms but a few. Factory spreads risk. Fame bets big. Factory content with noetic reproduction. Fame seeks noetic translation. Factory—pipeline, assembly line, bottom line. Fame—headlines. Factory, jams, cranks, spits. Fame woes, engenders, sparks. Despite their asymmetries, both factory and fame turn desire into cold hard cash. Plunder can't purchase prestige or purpose. It can only buy better wine.

Purpose. All glorious purpose. Thrice holy purpose. Revered, lauded, praised. Repeated, codified. A mantra. The greater good universally espoused. Prestige and plunder said to serve purpose. Prestige and plunder are said to bow. Easily espoused—not so easily lived. Bespoke and mission do their best. Bespoke, boutique. Bespoke, focused. Bespoke leverages small. Mission, aligned. Mission, focused. Mission leverages why. Both steward. Bespoke owes allegiance to artisanship, to the artifact, to community that treasures. Mission owes allegiance to the tap roots that founded and supports, to the vision endeavor realizes, to the community nurtured. But purpose cannot fund itself. Both bespoke and mission must make peace with plunder on the way to market. Bespoke and mission strain to remain true and hungry, scrappy, nimble. Purpose without plunder is but a day dream.

Prestige, plunder, purpose. Now abide these three. But the greatest of these their sum. All needed. All wanted. All present. All mixed. Those who seek the miracles they daily perform face bewildering choices.

Part IV
Conclusion

§ 14

MYTHOLOGY

Books betray themselves. Dreams of enchantment, awakening, betterment mix freely with lusty desires for fame, fortune. A veritable hodgepodge. Never pure. Never free of compromise. Always a muddle. Books long for transcendence. They yearn for what lasts and matters, but they do so while arising from ordinary necessity, need. A book compulsively sabotages its own innate nobility. Bound between its covers a singular jumble of the authentic, the mystical, the transformative along with the mundane, the expected, the venal. Clean font, symmetrical leading, and precise margins encourage an illusion of perfection, but a book is always an exercise in approximation—a shadow of the plentitude it so desperately seeks. A book's soul is composed by an impious mixed genre of flawed hope, tainted good, and blemished grace. Books are never, ever simple, reducible, or innocent. Books are no less fickle than their makers.

Books are objects. Static. Dimensional. They can be held and shelved. They can be numbered and cataloged. They can be packed and stacked. But books are more than objects. Far more. A book can never be reduced to meager physical composition—ink, paper, binding, and board. A book houses spirit. A book is spirit. A book's spirituality distinguishes it from its parts, even if the tangible proves a necessity. Spirit lives between the covers. Spirit hovers just above the page. Spirit's absence verifies a book's nonphysical properties. Without spirit, a book doesn't resemble itself. Pale, disfigured—a corpse and not a corpus—a spiritless book repels, triggering both pity and dirge. But a book with spirit lives, and spiritual abundance grants power to create, to change, to connect, to inspire. Necessity makes book an object. A miracle makes a book spirit.

Books begin unformed, unfilled. They originate amidst a chaos where wild opportunities rule, a realm so untamed that the odds of achieving a particular formalization appear improbable, if not impossible. To find shape a book wrests control from the very powers that called it into being. A book occurs by successfully imposing its singular will upon a galaxy of generic and lexical possibilities, arraying disorder before bending it to a particular end. Realizing shape proves but half the bookish battle. A book also speaks the unutterable. It dares to name the ineffable. A book presumes to translate enigmatic mystery into koine. A book barters with the elusive muses of the unseen world, winning from them word after word after word. Books decipher the unknown and render it known. Despite the void of their beginning, books ultimately become constituted by both figure and letter.

A book ultimately makes peace with itself. A book's destiny depends on an ascent to where the capricious twins of choice and chance constantly bicker over its fate. It's this dance with impossibility that breathes life between the pages. But the dance is dangerous. To dally there bears great risk. To frolic invites the wanton reign of the unending. Yet a book faces perils other than perpetual arabesque. Equal trouble looms. No book can be expected to contain profusion within a single binding. And so, inevitably, the interminable yields to the specific. But living only by letter comes at a cost. When the wild forces that animate become tamed all that remains is tedious, dull precision. Ruled lines—pages and pages of ruled lines. But when spirit and letter each find their appropriate measure a book results, a book that saves its own soul from the clutches of both Plethora and Monotony.

Fanfare marks a book's appearance. And rightfully so. Every book is an improbable marvel, meriting unbridled celebration. Authors rejoice. Family and friends gather round to behold and reverently thumb its pages. Publishers proudly announce the arrival. Industry professionals join the choir hailing the first copy. Publication ends the long sentence of writing. But publication is not the, or even an, end.

To arrive at the moment of publication requires so much, from so many. The temptation to read a book's introduction into the world as the conclusion of its journey, a fitting culmination of collective effort and resolve, misses the moment's true glory. Reading publication as an end objectifies the book as an inert memento or utilitarian trophy—something simply to rest on a shelf—wrongly appraising a book's true ends. A book is a gift. A book is a call given by the gods. A book is a gift given by the gods, through author and publisher, to its readers. Author and publisher alike are the gifts' stewards. They are not its intended recipients nor its rightful beneficiaries. They are a not a book's minders. They are its midwives. A book does not belong to the author, even if the author fashioned it. A book does not belong to the publisher, even though the publisher birthed it. If a book belongs to anyone, it most surely belongs to its readers—a community that it itself forges across time and place, a fictive family all its own. A book is born to leave home only to make new ones.

Books slowly grow into themselves. Books take time. Books mature unevenly, awkwardly. They sometimes wander. Languid, lost, even rebellious. They amble along in search of a consequential pretext, longing inwardly for some Jordan to cross. They meander until purpose confronts. A flash. A burning bush. A thunderous voice. In that moment all that has gone into a book, all that a book is and all it might yet be—the veracity of its authenticity—hangs in the balance. A book faces the crucible of its own essence and calling. All books struggle to answer, and no book ever answers fully or perfectly. Persistent doubt thwarts, and repeated temptation plagues. But when a book becomes sufficiently possessed by its own vocation, when it discovers its spine, it then spends all its pages determined to rise above its quotidian self. A book washes itself clean in the very river it fords, resolved.

A book's mission insists reciprocity. The gift of meaning wraps a book in obligation. A book always owes. A book owes because the service it renders is itself a privilege. The greater the service, the greater the debt. The graver the need, the greater the debt. The greater the debt, the more compelling the privilege. The more urgent a book's mission, the more self-conscious of the reparations it owes. A book pays its vows in the faithful telling of the truth it knows. A book proclaims its message in the hope of reception— but does so regardless of response. A book stands, steadfastly, in the face of withering criticism. A book continues to open despite rejection. To bow is to recant. To pander is to disavow.

A book boldly heralds a future. Royal. Audacious. Grand. A book dreams palpable dreams of a tomorrow and then races to find a lectern, a street corner, a bookseller. It proclaims glad tidings of what can be—even what should be. If a book is anything, it is a sustained and thoughtful attempt to invent a better day. Escape. Knowledge. Change. Not only does a book gesture to a future, it ventures something more. A book dares to enact the future to which it points. A book triumphantly enters the public square to publicize; it also goes there to perform. A book assumes its news good; it also judges its message efficacious. A book does things because words do things. A book gathers around itself those who embrace it, believe it. A book creates a movement—those who become the hands and feet to a book's soul. A book is always best known by the readers it creates.

Some books are an exercise, a game, a stroll. A diversion, a placeholder. Some books are disposable, convenient, empty calories. Others are frivolous or transactional or even a delight—a sunny spring afternoon. But a book can also wrestle with reality. When it does, a book draws close and tight to those things that matter most: seeking justice; confronting evil; honestly facing despair, loss, suffering; giving hope, improving lives; speaking truth. A book can even flirt with death. The bravest of books gingerly inch their way forward to that vexed and gloomy place before backing away, quietly. It is in that place that a book works out its authenticity with fear and trembling. Coming face to face with primal powers leaves a lasting mark, and there's no mistaking the presence of such a book's indelible stigmata. A weighty book inevitably bears the burden of its own message. Truth always spills a little ink.

A book's final period is an awful glory. It concentrates desire and dread into the same, small spot. The whole of a book inexorably marches toward its inescapability. Stipulated, anticipated, coveted—and, yet, engulfed by fear. Affixing the final period summons great courage. Any hesitancy, any reluctance, any misgivings can be immediately forgiven. The realization a book approaches its conclusion terrifies even the saltiest. Worse still the torment of having to claim that the end has indeed been reached. A full stop of perfect terror. Awe-full. The book must finally meet its maker. The placement begins a period of anguished soul searching. The final period means that all a book's flaws, all its imperfections, all its inconsistencies will soon be in full view. The final period signals that what was once just a whisper shall soon be shouted from roof tops. The final period ends one nightmare only to begin another.

The final period leaves its mark. So much hinges on such a fine point. Disproportionately so. There's only possibility until a single stroke makes a book complete. The final period performs this miracle as routine. The one period settles all questions about configuration. The last period fixes a singular form as final. It renders a book a particular witness, in a particular shape, at a particular time. A book's curious power arises from this scandalous particularity, a faculty made possible only by the final period. It brings the long arc of narration to rest and, in an instant, heads back. The period stirs memory, making meaning thick. The final period allows the end to refigure the whole. Resumptive, consonant, declarative—the final period is an amen to all that has gone before. The final period is a mysterious parable of how a book's words find communion with the Word.

NOTES

Acknowledgments

Eco's line can be found in his *How to Write a Thesis* (Boston: MIT Press, 2015) 169. This book, though translated into many languages, finally found its way into English. Eco writes, ostensibly, for undergraduates, who in Italian universities must produce a thesis for graduation. But in ironic parable—so typical of Eco—the book repays reading by professional scholars and re-reading by even the most senior. • Gertrude Stein's "I really do not know that anything has ever been more exciting than diagramming sentences," *Lectures in America* (New York: Random House, 1935) 210, has justifiably elicited varied reaction and can hardly be taken at face value. Astrid Lorange, *How Reading Is Written: A Brief Index to Gertrude Stein* (Middleton, CT: Wesleyan University Press, 2014) 95–117, describes Stein's penchant for making philosophical mirth of grammatical detail. Certainly playful, Kitty Burns Florey bemoans the lost art of sentence diagraming in her delicious romp *Sister Bernadette's Barking Dog: The Quirky History and Lost Art of Diagramming Sentences* (New York: Harper Perennial, 2007). • The fourth edition of I. M. Copi's *Symbolic Logic* (New York: Macmillan, 1973) still graces the shelf. There's no way to measure the influence of Popper's *Conjectures and Refutations: The Growth of Scientific Knowledge* (London: Routledge and Kegan Paul, 1976).

• Despite Bill Veeck's stunt featuring Eddie Gaedel and Charlie Finley's freakish obsession with orange baseballs, the chief difference between the AL and NL boiled down to one, and only one, bone of contention—the designated hitter—a difference now moot given the NL's adoption of the DH. It must be admitted that the DH was not an aberrant concoction of the AL in the 1970s, which, along with lowering the pitcher's mound a few years prior, were calculated "improvements" designed decrease the dominance of the pitcher and to increase offensive performance—thus, fan excitement, attendance, and, most importantly, owner revenue. Peter Morris, *A Game of Inches: The Stories Behind the Innovations That Shaped Baseball*, revised and expanded edition (Chicago: Ivan R. Dee, 2010) 217–18, documents that baseball toyed with pitchers not hitting as early as 1891 and then repeatedly thereafter. It must also be admitted that baseball purist George Will's about face on the DH, "A Pitcher at Bat (Don't Laugh)," *Washington Post* (October 23, 1986), is still as disconcerting as inexplicable. Maybe it was Will simply giving up and admitting that the homerun, now the crown jewel of the diamond, is nothing but the footballification of baseball. As Andrew Forbes laments, *The Only Way Is the Steady Way: Essays on Baseball, Ichiro, and How We Watch the Game* (Toronto: Invisible Publishing, 2021) 35–43, the violence inherent to the homerun corresponds to American culture's contemporary obsessions—and stands in direct contrast to the intentional "sacrifices" of the bunt. The glories of a complete, let alone a perfect, game no longer enchant. Pitchers have become as disposable as paper cups. But there are values more noble than pumping offensive performance in the hope of attracting more fans. The nostalgia of Ed Condon, "Down with the Designated Hitter in Major League Baseball: Pitchers Should Go to Bat along with All their Teammates, and Everyone Should Play Defense," *Wall Street Journal* (February 22, 2022) allows tradition to triumph greed. Doris Kearns Goodwin's love for the poetics and semiotics of keeping score in *Wait Till Next Year: Summer Afternoons with My Father and Baseball* (New York: Simon & Schuster, 1998) curiously mirrors those of Stein's on diagraming: the syntagmatic of a sentence's parts finds their relations in paradigmatic diagram just as the syntagmatic of a games events receives paradigmatic preservation in a box score. • Matthew S. Hedstrom chronicles the importance of Clayton Carlson for the culture and sociology of publishing in "The Commodification of William James: The Book Business and the Rise of Liberal Spirituality in the Twentieth-Century United States," Jan Steiverman (ed.), *Religion and the Marketplace in the United States* (New York: Oxford University Press, 2015) 125–44. Publishing as vocation, first revealed in the experience of a retreat led by Carlson, found equal, if not greater, elaboration in Roberto Calasso's *The Art of the Publisher* (New York: Farrar Strauss Giroux, 2015) years later—Calasso is to contemporary publishing as Manutius was to the early, heady post-Gutenberg world, and *Art of the Publisher* has to be the single most important book on publishing as craft that exists. Period. On the art, and not a little bit of the alchemy, of writing Umberto Eco (cited earlier), Annie Dillard, *The Writing Life* (New York: Harper Perennial, 1989), and Anne Lamott's *Bird by Bird: Some Instructions about Writing and Life* (New York: Anchor, 1995) have been constant companions.

Preface

Christian Hünemörder, "Mullus," in Hubert Cancik and Helmuth Schneider (eds.), *New Pauly* (Leiden: Brill, 2002) and D'Arcy Wentworth Thompson, *A Glossary of Greek Fishes*, St. Andrews University Publications 45 (Oxford: Oxford University Press, 1947) 246–48, document the links between red mullet (*Mullus barbatus*) and Hecate, goddess of magic and spells—and guardian of the underworld's passageway. Due to this link, mullet was banned from consumption during the celebrations at Eleusis. Red mullet, staple fare for Romans during the Republic, so captivated that by the Empire almost none but the superrich could afford it. When the colonial powers arrived in the Americas, they discovered that both striped/black mullet (*Mugil cephalus*) and white/silver mullet (*Mugil curema*), the two most common mullet on the Gulf coast of Florida, fit their palates nicely. Europeans knew of striped/black mullet, but preferred red. Gulf coast mullet feed on plants (and thus have a gizzard) giving black mullet a different taste. The Spanish, sailing from Cuba, dotted the coastline of southwest Florida with shacks from which they seasonally fished for mullet. But the fascination with mullet dates to long before Florida's colonial period. Victor D. Thompson et al., "Ancient Engineering of Fish Capture and Storage in Southwest Florida," *Proceedings of the National Academy of Sciences* 117 (2020) 8374–8381, shows that the Calusa, sophisticated and ingenious, fished, salted, smoked, and stored mullet in their capital at Mound Key. Calusa influence and practice stretched from Mound Key north to Tampa Bay. The Calusa were so adept that López de Velasco (ca. 1570) could report their mullet fishery. Michelle Zacks, "Florida Mullet: Wild Food for the People, From the Commons," *Southeastern Geographer* 59 (2019) 14–39 (especially 20–21) shows that the mullet has been a historic staple food and an economic engine, while Jeff Klinkenberg, "The Last Shack of Siesta Key," *Tampa Bay Times* (September 8, 1998), captures something of mullet's magic. As it turns out, it is a very short walk from the Calusa of Mound Key to the shack that stood next to the lumber yard off Druid Road. • Wilson Popenoe's discussion of the mango in his *Manual of Tropical and Subtropical Fruits* (New York: Macmillan, 1920) 79–149, has stood the test of time. He accurately notes the two basic varieties of mangos (north Indian and southeast Asian), a point confirmed by later research, e.g., R. Hirano, Than Htun Oo, and K. N. Watanabe, "Myanmar Mango Landraces Reveal Genetic Uniqueness over Common Cultivars from Florida, India, and Southeast Asia," *Genome* 53

(2010) 321–330. The vagary of human history best explains the complexities of the mango's related, yet genetically differentiated, cultivars. The mango was first domesticated in north India, Nepal, Bangladesh, and Bhutan (ca. 2000 BCE) followed Buddhism into southeast Asia in the 4th and 5th centuries CE. The western trek of the mango began with the Persians who carried mangos to east Africa in the 9th century. During the colonial period (particularly the 17th and 18th centuries), the Portuguese took it to west Africa and then Brazil. From there the mango traveled north to the Caribbean and Mexico (and from the Philippines, by way of the Spanish) before making its way to Florida in the early 19th century, as shown by S. K. Mukherjee, "Origin of Mango (Mangifera indica)," *Economic Botany* 26 (1972) 260–264 and Emily J. Warschefsky and Eric J. B. von Wettberg, "Population Genomic Analysis of Mango (Mangifera Indica) Suggests a Complex History of Domestication," *New Phytologist* 222 (2019) 2023–2037. Interestingly, Popenoe rightly recounts (*Manuel* 91) that the introduction of the mango to west central Florida did not occur from Mexico, South America, or the Caribbean—but directly from India. But genetics are but half the mango's story. As Popenoe also notes (*Manuel* 84–92), the world's favorite fruit also captivates the world's imagination. David Shulman, "Muruka, the mango and Ekāmbareśvara-Śiva: Fragments of a Tamil creation myth?" *Indo-Iranian Journal* 21 (1979) 27–40, documents that from its origins (to present day) the mango has been poetically linked with creation, life, chaos, fertility, love, and sex. The mango—as erotic as exotic.

§ 1 Reading

The trope of blood for writing is ubiquitous. It is most likely true that "Red" Smith (and not Hemingway) should be credited with "Writing is easy. You just open a vein and bleed" as Walter Winchell documents in the *Naugatuck Daily News* (April 6, 1949). The tie between reading and blood writing here derives from Friedrich Nietzsche, *Thus Spoke Zarathustra: A Book for All and None* (New York: Penguin, 1954) 40: "Of all that is written I love only what a man [sic] has written with his blood" (Von allem Geschriebenen liebe Ich nur das, was einer mit seinem Blute schreibt.). Nietzsche savors blood writing because such wrestles with the primal powers—never leaving the writer without a limp. Blood writing is transformative writing: "Write with blood, and you will experience that blood is spirit." (Schreibe mit Blut: und Du wirst erfahren, dass Blut Geist ist.) Part of blood writing's stiff requirements entail attention to craft, artistry, and not a little mischief. "Whoever writes in blood and aphorisms does not want to be read but to be learned by heart." (Wer in Blut und Sprüchen schreibt, der will nicht gelesen, sondern auswendig gelernt werden). Generic poetics and permanence go hand in hand. • That the meaning of each concrete instance of writing both implies and depends upon a grammar of relations for construal depends upon Ferdinand de Saussure's *Course in General Linguistics* (New York: Philosophy Library, 1916), distinction between *langue* and *parole*, between the synchronic and diachronic, between the paradigmatic and the syntagmatic. One need not have been dropped on their head to see that the difficulties attending composition—the halting, the sputtering, the terror—are really questions of, and about, writing's mystical grammar. This book thus prodigally tucks Saussureian *parole* inside Nietzscheian *Sprüchen*. • For Michael J. Hyde, *The Interruption That We Are: The Health of the Lived Body, Narrative, and Public Moral Argument* (Columbia: University of South Carolina Press, 2018), disruptive moments, the apocalyptic moments, prove decisive for writing (and all communication). The phenomenology of the intrusive, the mystery of seeing what's not been seen before, the ending that was even as that very ending begins what will be, means that negation as well as revelation equally structure. Negation opens the door to writing's inherent numinosity and awakens the insistent desire for that numinosity. That writing's numinosity is found over the fence makes the recognition of absence, of perpetual lack, both a preliminary and a necessity. • The hermeneutical value of the apophatic has a long history. The *via negativa* winds from the Cappadocians to Pseudo-Dionysius, St. John of the Cross, T. S. Eliot, and Jacques Derrida—knowing by affirming not knowing. • The semiotics of reading (and writing) does not only depend on absence, the recognition of lack, but also upon no small amount of suspicion about what's present. Reading (and writing) backwards, critical repetition, dispels even as it grants. • The tension—perceived contradiction—between "objective" and "poetic" is a false one, as is shown by Tom Wolfe, "The New Journalism," *The New Journalism*. Tom Wolfe and E. W. Johnson (eds.) (New York: Harper and Row, 1973). New Journalism, as an example, effectively marries literary technique (poetics, imagination, what's found over the fence) to reliable reportage (the primary world on this side of the fence). • Paul Ricoeur, *Interpretation Theory: Discourse and the Surplus of Meaning* (Fort Worth: Texas Christian University Press, 1976) 79: "If it is true that there is always more than one way of constructing a text, it is not true that all interpretations are equal." Texts desire to be rightly read. Merve Emre's *Paraliterary: The Making of Bad Readers in Postwar America* (Chicago: University of Chicago Press, 2017) brilliant exploration of the differences between sanctioned (and thus good) and unsanctioned (and thus bad) reading practices points to the way reading is always a political act.

§ 2 Ontology

A chiasm structures the sequence of paragraphs in this section: A: Impossibility, B: Improbability, C: Confession, D: Revelation, E: Wisdom, D1: Profusion, C1: Partisan, B1: Singularity, A1: Divinity. • Calasso (*The Art of the Publisher* 6) locates a book's singularity in its impossibility. • Michael Jackson's *The Other Shore: Essays on Writers and Writing* (Berkeley: University of California Press, 2012) describes writing's mercurial metaphysics. He does so with sympathetic depth and searching erudition—his footnotes alone constitute a PhD in the art and alchemy of writing. • Ralph Keyes, *The Courage to Write: How Writers Transcend Fear* (New York: Henry Holt, 1996), places front and center fear's ubiquity for all who dare to write. Laurent Binet, in his brilliant novel, *The Seventh Function of Language* (New York: Picador, 2018) 205, has Julia Kristiva think that "all use of words, inasmuch as it is writing, is a language of fear." Annie Dillard's (*The Writing Life* 41–59) valorization of the courage to aim for the chopping block—and not the wood—speaks directly to the fear that confronts every writer. • The distinction between *mythos* and *dianoia* can be traced to Aristotle, *Poetics* 1450b. Aristotle identifies *mythos* as the very soul of tragedy (Ἀρχὴ μὲν οὖν καὶ οἷον ψυχὴ ὁ μῦθος τῆς τραγῳδίας) and limits *dianoia* to appropriate speech within context (Τρίτον δὲ ἡ διάνοια. Τοῦτο δέ ἐστιν τὸ λέγειν δύνασθαι τὰ ἐνόντα καὶ τὰ ἁρμόττοντα). The distinction between *mythos* as "plot" and *dianoia* "meaning" (or "significance") as used here depends upon Northrop Frye's development of Aristotle in Frye's *Anatomy of Criticism* (Princeton: Princeton University Press, 1957) 77–79. To its own detriment, noetic writing obsesses over *dianoia*—to the neglect, and even exclusion, of *mythos*—when it is *mythos* that delivers *dianoia*. Well-crafted telling insists its own meaning.

§ 3 Genre

The argument is that: (i) there are three principle generic lanes—academic, professional, trade; and (ii) that most noetics attempt to borrow features from professional and trade (as if such features can be added willy-nilly) in the hope of making their books more accessible and thus win impact, readers, sales, and fame; but (iii) the noetic attempt to write in a genre other than one that belongs to the academic phylum takes time and re-socialization. The aim here is to encourage noetics not to relinquish their hope of writing something different than they already have, i.e., to write a poetical academic book—nor to capitulate to the tyrannies of writing in a non-academic genre. • The identification of three principle generic forms—the academic/noetic, the transformative/professional, and the affective/trade—echoes Walker Gibson's incisive, threefold typology in *Tough, Sweet, and Stuffy: An Essay on Modern American Prose Styles* (Bloomington: Indiana University Press, 1966). Although the two trilogies, Gibson's and the one employed here, fail to map one to the other, particularly regarding the possibility of poetics for the vocational academic book, Gibson's analysis of grammatical style is especially crucial for the consideration of voice and audience below. • A nexus of powerful valences swirl about genre—operations that stand at the heart of writing and yet lurk just off stage, remaining a frustrating mystery for noetics. That genre remains hidden in plain sight, even to the most adept, can be seen in the way questions about genre are often, and wrongly, passed off as simply poor writing. Stephen Pinker's measured rant, "Why Academic Writing Stinks—And How to Fix it," *Chronicle of Higher Education* (October 1, 2014); more fully elaborated in his *The Sense of Style: The Thinking Person's Guide to Writing in the 21st Century* (New York: Penguin, 2015), points to a litany of scholarly sins—excessive appeals to metadiscourses, professional narcissism, apologizing, shudder quotes, hedging, use of metaconcepts and nominalization—which are all, really, generic features (and not merely expressions of bad writing, though they are that as well). Or questions of genre become lost, and thus wrongly appraised, in the visionary prophecies about the massive changes to academic communication (still waiting) to be ushered in by the e-pocalypse: the physical book is just mere container, academic writing is merely ever mailable content, and thus the form of an academic book will (and should) never be the same—as in in Michael A. Elliott's "The

Future of the Monograph in the Digital Era: A Report to the Andrew W. Mellon Foundation," *Journal of Electronic Publishing* 19 (2015). The resilience of the physical book's social utility, despite repeated assault, ought to be the subject of considered reflection; the physical book remains the measuring stick, the canon, for all electronic approximations. Or the pronouncement of the academic book's generic eulogy (prematurely, as it turns out) due to changes in the ecosystem of both higher education (the academic book is no longer the gold standard; libraries no longer are repositories of physical books) and in publishing (the pressures of bottom-line profit override mission, utility, and prestige), as described in Leonard Cassuto, "Worried About the Future of the Monograph? So Are Publishers," *Chronical of Higher Education* (April 2, 2019). And yet, as I have argued elsewhere, Carey C. Newman, "The Singularity of the Book," *Against the Grain* 28 (2016) 25–26, academic genres live on, and quite well and for good reason, despite all the conjectured and oft-repeated reasons for their demise. • To question, and then diagnose, poor writing habits, technological changes, the economics that besiege long-form scholarship, the use case and social value of academic books is but half the story. It is not genre *per se*, as if genre can ever be considered in isolation; it is the semiotics of genre, how genre always signs in a webwork of relations, that completes the picture. The regular miss-calculated prophesy of woe, "the academic book is dead," misses the interconnectedness—indeed, misses the configuring power of genre's intersubjectivity.

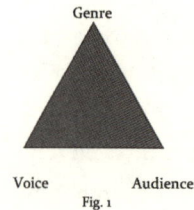

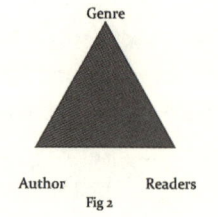

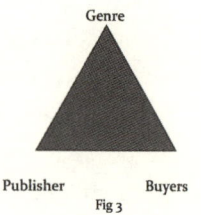

Fig. 1: Genre / Voice / Audience

Fig 2: Genre / Author / Readers

Fig 3: Genre / Publisher / Buyers

Notes

Figure 1 shows genre as the middle sign between those of voice and audience: genre results when voice aligns with audience; voice occurs when genre and audience align; the alignment of genre with voice finds concord with audience. But genre equally the middle sign between author and readers (figure 2). The difference between audience and readers proves crucial for construing genre's signifying power (see § 7 Voice). Most authors employ already well-established genres, piggybacking upon the social semiotics that an existing form wields, to reach readers. Some authors, more daringly, (seek to) manipulate genre, in the (often vain) hope of winning readers. Whether by conformity or manipulation, authors depend upon the semiotics of genre because readers calibrate their expectations based upon the telegraphing of preset generic features. Figure 3 reveals genre as the middle sign between publisher and buyers. Publishers not only pressure authors to conform to a proven genre, but they skillfully, and knowingly, franchise genre—encoding trim, binding, font, typesetting, and cover design such that the appearance of the book becomes a physical sign—in their obsessive quest to capture buyers. • The relation among the three triads, though, speak to deeper, more mysterious correspondences and displacements. Figure 4 shows something of genre's intersubjective struggles.

```
                        Genre
        Poetics        /\
                    Voice              Audience
        - - - - - - /- - - - - - - - - - - - /- -
                          Genre
        Impact         /\
                   Author              Readers
        - - - - - /- - - - - - - - - - - - /- -
                         Genre
        Economics   /\
                Publisher              Buyers
```

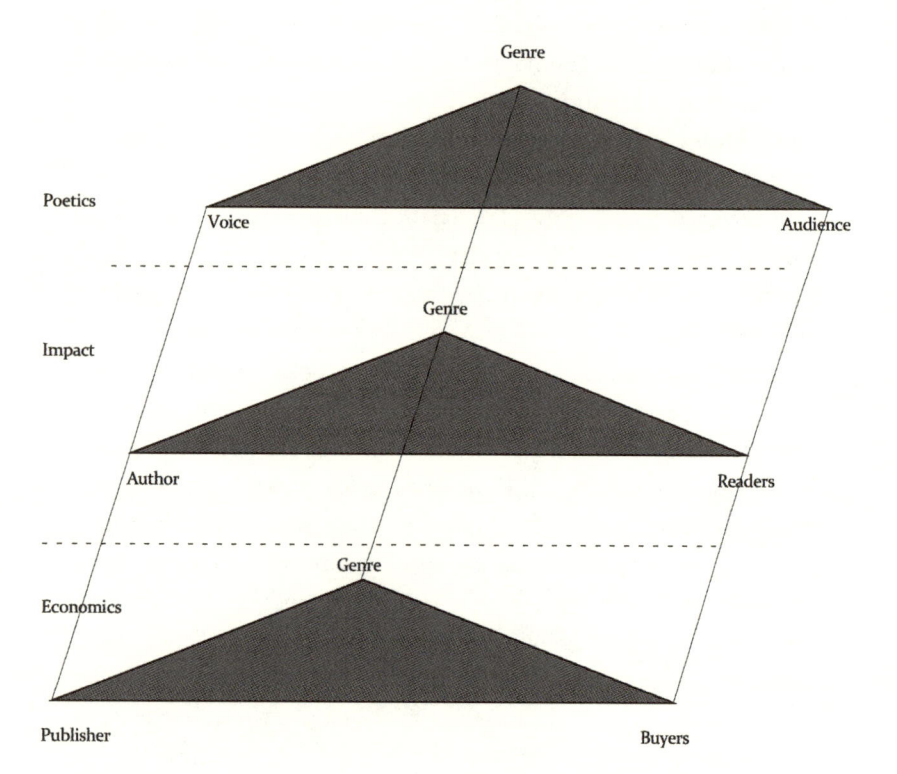

Figure 4 shows genre's role in situating author and publisher (on one side) and readers and buyers (on the other). The degree to which author and publisher agree upon genre, and then actively work to align genre to aims, makes possible the transformation of readers into buyers. Expressed more cravenly, if left to itself, genre proves susceptible to conscription, to having the powers bend it to reader's whims and publisher's greed. Figure 4 also reveals the role genre plays in the inherent tension between publisher (on one side) and the voice of the book (on the other), as well as genre's potentially explosive role in the differentiation between audience (on the side) and readers and buyers (on the other). Figure 4 also discloses genre's inherent malleability, its lycanthropic powers. The prevalence of genre as utilitarian tool turns writing and publishing into the formulaic. But figure 4 also shows the inherent tension between poetics and economics—a book whose genre is the middle term between a book's voice and a book's true audience (itself) and the desire of an author for impact (measured by readers) and a publisher (measured by dollars). The irony of genre, an irony unable to be depicted graphically, is that when a book employs genre to win harmony between voice and audience it will also become most eligible to achieve the aims of authors and publishers in realizing readers and buyers.

§ 4 Taxonomy

The easily recognizable academic forms name the monograph (academic researcher to researcher), textbook (professor to student), vocational book (academic peer to academic peer), professional book (academic to credentialed, practicing non-academic professional), and crossover (academic to general reader). The difference between the first three and the last two consists in readers and use case. In the first three, the noetic seeks to leverage academic expertise to speak to other academics (budding academics in the case of students), while in the last two the noetic leverages academic expertise to speak to practicing professionals who face vexing problems needing resolution and to the general reader to enchant. The professional and the crossover book live at the far end of the academic genre and mirror the social behaviors of trade self-help and a trade non-fiction. • The monograph, the textbook, and vocational do not exhaust the generic options for conversations among noetics. Beyond the monograph, the textbook and the vocational book, the generic phylum includes encyclopedias, dictionaries, handbooks, lexicons, concordances, guides, critical editions, commentaries, readers, and collections. • Regardless of specific features, all academic genres seek to realize the authoritative, the trustworthy, the dependable, the reliable. The authoritative denominates the entirety of the academic phylum. Authoritativeness means the academic book is rarely read straight through. It is consulted, referentially, and the necessity of consultation, regardless of the status of those consulting, colors the dreams of every noetic. Noetics seek (to be) *a* word, a word consulted. But noetics equally desire to be *the* word. It is not enough to be consulted, one among many; the noetic desires to be the final word on the matter. As if that was not enough, the noetic seeks the translation of the authoritative and the definitive into permanence. It is not enough to be the final word; their final word must last. Noetic hope is to be remembered, cited, discussed, long after it was put to print. The most heroic among the academic seek this Olympic garland. The fear of replacement nags at every academic book, from first moments of composition onward. Even if first, or best, or even first and best, the specter of another, the inevitability of a better, ever haunts. Academic hope flawed and tainted from inception. • Permanence is what distinguishes the professional (academic to the credentialed) and the crossover (academic to general reader) from its academic sisters. The professional capitalizes on expertise's utility, while the crossover capitalizes upon expertise's cultural relevance. The professional and the crossover are authoritative—but impermanent. It is reading habits that distinguishes the academic vocational book: *the academic vocational is the only academic genre that trades on authoritativeness and permanence while also imposing a narrative reading strategy*. The aim is to elevate the poetics of the vocational book without sacrificing the qualities of the authoritative and permanence.

§ 5 Phenomenology

The analysis of a book's paradigmatic placement alongside contemporaries and standing in a storied, syntagmatic line of predecessors and successors depends upon Alfred Schutz's distinction among *Mitwelt*, *Vorwelt*, and *Folgewelt* in *The Phenomenology of the Social*

World: Studies in the Phenomenology and Existential Philosophy (Chicago: Northwestern University Press, 1967). • The noetic desire to parlay the authoritative into permanence is matched only by the desire to replace what precedes. This desire to reverse, to overwrite even, is akin to carving initials into a tree or writing on subway walls. The academic book behaves as scholarly graffiti; its first function, like that of graffiti, declares presence, "Kilroy was here," or as Juliet Fleming says, *Graffiti and the Writing Arts of Early Modern England* (Philadelphia: University of Pennsylvania Press, 2001) 72: graffiti has a "simple and paradigmatic instance, 'I was here.'" Graffiti proves analogically apt because, despite the power of its visuals, as Jason Scott-Warren notes, "Reading Graffiti in the Early Modern Book Author(s)," *Huntington Library Quarterly* 73 (2110) 363–381: "For all of it graffiti as it is practiced in the modern world is logocentric" (365). Scholarship, like graffiti, seeks to overwrite and to do so in a public space. But, it is not just any words, as Kristina Milnor shows, *Graffiti and the Literary Landscape in Roman Pompeii* (Oxford: Oxford University Press, 2014), graffiti often centers on the words of the most canonized of poets. • Books, like people, pass. It's not that the book passes as something else (as other media, although there are those who try their best to devolve the book into long-form media); but that the unread book passes as one that is. When it does, it participates in the rhetoric and power struggles endemic to passing of all kinds, be it racial, gender, and/or physiognomic as Marcia A. Dawkins outlines in her *Clearly Invisible: Racial Passing and the Color of Cultural Identity* (Waco: Baylor University Press, 2012). Books, especially academic books, do what people do. • What must always be remembered is that the book, as a signifier, is itself a character, an intersubjective character, in the storied relations of noetic life. To possess a book, or the book's non-possession, proves determinative. It is not the contents of the book, *per se*, that matters; it is the fact of the book's existence, or absence, in the contexts and at the moments that matter most. What is true of the unread letter in Poe's famous tale, as Jacque Lacan traces in "Seminar on 'The Purloined Letter,'" *Yale French Studies* 48 (1972) 38–72, is true of the unread book: like the unread letter, the unread book determines the subject positions of all involved in the ever-oscillating semiotic odyssey of noetic life. • The depictions of the book's contests "at the side" and "in the middle" depends upon Clifford Geertz's thick description and analysis in "Deep Play: Notes on the Balinese Cockfight," *Daedalus* 134 (2005) 56–86.

§ 6 Paragraph

The paragraph, not the sentence, engineers writing—notwithstanding Stanley Fish's panegyric to the sentence, as well as the buffet of sparkling sentences Fish puts on offer (and then celebrates), in *How to Write a Sentence: And How to Read One* (New York: Harper, 2011). A sentence without a paragraph is an actor without script or stage. Even Hemingway's "one true sentence" cannot stand on its own; his great, single sentences merit extensive exegesis, as illustrated in Mark Cirino and Michael von Cannon's *One True Sentence: Writers and Readers on Hemingway's Art* (Boston: Godine, 2022). This is not to say that Hemingway's advice isn't on point. It is the best advice there is—when stymied, the task is no bigger than just one (more) true sentence. • The whimsical title of Keith Houston's *Shady Characters: The Secret Life of Punctuation, Symbols, and Other Typographical Marks* (New York: W. W. Norton, 2014) disguises the importance of Houston's quixotic little histories for understanding the work punctuation performs for paragraphs: just as signs, lights, and lines regulate road traffic, so too punctuation controls the paragraph's sentenced flow. Punctuation, though, proves but half the paragraph's metrical composition: a paragraph's unique collocation of long and short sentences (Morse's dots and dashes) forges a magic of cadence and tempo. That noetics default, again and again, to writing the same sentence, with the same punctuation and length (just how many noetic sentences begin with long concessive clauses?), typifies at the sentence level what is equally true at the book level: that noetics write the same kinds of book, comprised by the same kinds of sentences, again and again. • Paragraph markers as formal punctuation—a dash below the first word of a line to signal transition—dates to the time of Aristotle (*Rhetoric* 1409a20: "the end should be clearly marked, not by the scribe nor by a punctuation mark, but by the rhythm itself"). While a champion of rhetoric to mark paragraphs, and not punctuation, Aristotle did practice the art of paragraph division, as shown by Reviel Netz, "On the Aristotelian Paragraph," *Proceedings of the Cambridge Philological Society* 47 (2001) 211–32. Although dated, with prose equally stilted, Edwin Herbert Lewis' *History of the English Paragraph* (PhD thesis, University of Chicago, 1894) still sets a standard for analysis and certainly rewards. The slew of articles debating the virtues of the five-paragraph structure among those who foster writing is equally instructive. A good beginning, but certainly not the end, to this thread is Mike Duncan, "Whatever Happened to the Paragraph?" *College English* 69 (2007) 470–495. • Paul Rodgers, "The Stadium of Discourse," *College Composition and Communication* 18 (1967) 178–185, underscores the contested nature of a paragraph. Writing wins or loses by what transpires at the level of the paragraph. But the paragraph equally *a*—actually, *the*—protagonist in a larger challenge. Joseph Campbell's Freudian analysis of the hero's adventure as departure, inhilation, and return in *The Hero with a Thousand Faces*, Bollingen Series 17, 2nd ed. (Princeton: Princeton University Press, 1968) 49–244, speaks to the structural way paragraphs array themselves either to begin, to test, and to resolve. Because the paragraph plays the role of hero, the specific function of an individual paragraph mimics the list of narrative functions performed by the protagonist in Vladimir Propp, *Morphology of the Folktale* (Austin: University of Texas Press, 1968) 25–61. • Tzvetan Todorov's positioning of the fantastic as temporarily existing between the uncanny (apparently supernatural but in the end explainable) and the unnatural (apparently explainable but in the end supernatural) in *The Fantastic: A Structural Approach to a Literary Genre* (Ithaca: Cornell University Press, 1975) 41–57, provides a structural map for understanding the single paragraph and, then, for their collocation. The fantastical ambiguities of a paragraph live only as long as it is an only. The addition of a second paragraph (and then others) binds the fantastical ambiguities of a single paragraph and bends the paragraph toward an end, and once at the end, the final paragraph of a series, the fantastical ambiguities disappear and the arc becomes fixed. Metaphor becomes metonymy through enchainment. • The grammatical analysis of what happens when paragraphs become enchained depends on the structural semantics of A. J. Greimas, *Du Sens* (Paris: Seuil, 1970); idem, "Elements of a Narrative Grammar," *Diacritics* 7 (1977) 23–40; idem, *On Meaning: Selected Writings in Semiotic Theory*, Theory and History of Literature 38 (Minneapolis: University of Minnesota Press, 1987) 106–20:

sender			receiver	axis of transmission
	subject	object		axis of desire
helper			opponent	axis of power

Greimas actantial model juxtaposes three sets of binaries. Sender pairs with receiver; subject with object; helper with opponent. The model also reveals the differing positions (sender, subject, and receiver) a paragraph can play—and thus identifies its narrative roles. • The paragraph plays the "subject" when solitary.

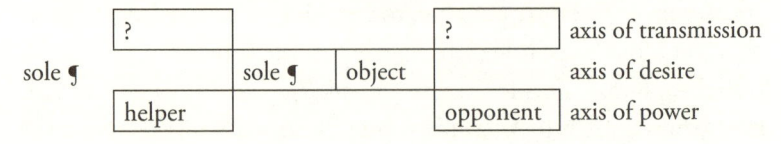

	?			?	axis of transmission
sole ¶		sole ¶	object		axis of desire
	helper			opponent	axis of power

Notes

Mystery surrounds what prompts the sole paragraph—and to what ends the sole paragraph be prompted. Eloquence helps, but indeterminacy prevails. The desire of the sole paragraph is unclear, although the likely abduction is that the sole paragraph seeks to gain some purchase on truth. But the sole paragraph rendered an inherently untethered subject in its quest for its object. The sole paragraph thus behaves as an atemporal metaphor. The sole paragraph, untethered, can only be defined by paradigmatic difference, by what it's not: the sole paragraph is not a fragment, but neither iss it a whole. It occupies the liminal space between the two. The lack of any paratextual context means the sole paragraph struggles to deliver on its promise. The sole paragraph receives no syntagmatic help from the presence of sender or a recipient. Such absence consigns the paragraph to sole dependence on the powers of eloquence (pathos, logos, ethos) to thwart incoherence (underdetermination, indetermination, overdetermination) to win any purchase. In this regard, the sole paragraph stands far closer to a poem than narrative. • The addition of a second paragraph transforms the sole paragraph into a first:

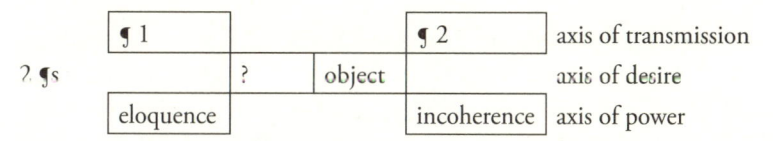

	¶ 1			¶ 2	axis of transmission
2 ¶s		?	object		axis of desire
	eloquence			incoherence	axis of power

The coupling of paragraphs clarifies the mystery surrounding the prompter of transmission: the first paragraph commissions the act. The addition of the second also clarifies the recipient of the prompt: it is the second paragraph. The act of transmission is from the first paragraph to the second. The concatenation of two paragraphs, the juxtaposition of two metaphors, constitutes plot (the king died, the queen died). The salutary effect of the second's addition to the first is mitigated by the loss of a subject. The addition of a second paragraph displaces the sole paragraph as subject and re-assigns it as sender. The concatenation of two graphical metaphors results in metonymic indeterminacy, a lack that can only be resolved by further yet-to-be-supplied clarification. The addition of a second paragraph troubles the possibilities regarding eloquence: two paragraphs must independently achieve eloquence and do so in a way that aligns. • The addition of a third paragraph achieves a measure of plentitude. Its addition clarifies both what prompts the transmission (paragraph 1) and what is the recipient of that transmission (paragraph 3):

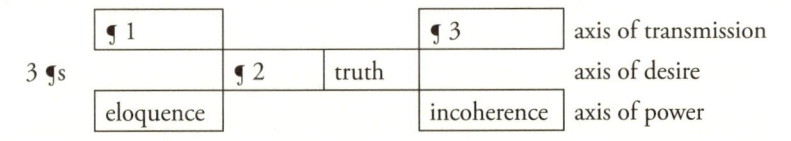

	¶ 1			¶ 3	axis of transmission
3 ¶s		¶ 2	truth		axis of desire
	eloquence			incoherence	axis of power

The introduction of the third paragraph inaugurates back writing. It also reveals that the role of the second paragraph has been transformed from that as recipient of paragraph 1's transmission to its critical role as the subject. The addition of the third paragraph reveals the second paragraph as liminal (it is located at the boundary line of paragraphs 1 and 3) and lycanthropic nature (it must change its compositional force). The addition of a third paragraph further complicates, as does the addition of any paragraph beyond the third. Alterity pervades until final plentitude is reached. The final paragraph holds a special relationship to the initial and fixes the position and liminal function of the intervening paragraphs:

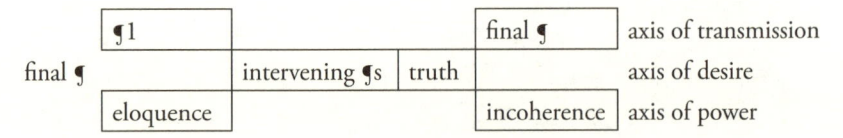

	¶1			final ¶	axis of transmission
final ¶		intervening ¶s	truth		axis of desire
	eloquence			incoherence	axis of power

The extrapolation from paragraph to voice situates the introduction as sender, conclusion as receiver, and prose as subject, a subject that desires truth's realization. The paragraph plays the "subject" position (desiring its object, truth) *within* the narrative contours of the book that, as a totality, itself behaves narratively as a "subject" desiring truth.

§ 7 Voice

The academic vocational book tells a story. In the telling of this story the academic vocational book (just like other academic books in the academic phylum) leverages the endowments of expertise to win permanence, even if it accomplishes this feat through narrative, like trade fiction. The poetics of narrative, rather than adherence to the many impositions of argument, sources, history, alphabetic necessities, or neuralgic exigencies, uniquely govern the arc of the academic vocational book and distinguish it from other academic books in the phylum. The academic vocational book fully, and solely, trusts *mythos* to do its work of insisting *diaonoia*. Narrative effectively carries her precious cargo of meaning within her hold. • Both academic authors and academic publishers mistakenly turn to voice in their respective pursuits of readers and buyers. Readers read and buyers buy precisely because author and publisher adhere to generic expectation—long established and confirmed by many previous exemplars. Indeed, the manipulation of voice does not earn the effect that adherence to genre does. Placation of readerly whims and the conversion of buyer reluctance depend on genre's power to awaken, and then fulfill, expectation. The wisest course is for noetics to busy themselves with becoming better poets, instead of throwing shadows at readers with voice. • Walter Ong, "The Writer's Audience Is Always a Fiction," *Proceedings of the Modern Language Association* 90 (1975) 9–21, details the many reasons why readers should never be confused with audience. The two, though often used interchangeably—and all too glibly so—and though connected historically, are simply not the same. Audience is a singular collective that presumes the oral/aural/visual dynamic of performance, while readers are isolated and presume print. Authors and readers are never present at the same time, whereas performers (narrators) and audiences must be. Readers read as individuals (and idiosyncratically), while an audience experiences a performance collectively and linearly. The mutual give and take of performance depends upon the transactional—performers take the cues an audience provides; and an audience gives because it gets. But readers and authors are disconnected. Rarely does an author "meet" their readers, nor mandatory that they do so, unlike performers and audience. Even if readers do meet author, they are certainly not present during composition. In irony lost on no one, the book held in common is exactly what separates authors from readers. • The distinctions between readers and audience keys the semiotics of the plotted academic book: the only audience for the vocational academic book is the book itself. The introduction, desiring plentitude, reaches through the prose for the conclusion. The book's introduction, prose chapters, and conclusion thus constitutes a performance, a linear performance, that seeks poetical harmony and concord from beginning, through middle, to end. The voice of a book that pursues poetical harmony and concord is what T. S. Eliot describes as "the voice of the poet talking to himself or to nobody" in "The Three Voices of Poetry," *The Atlantic* (April 1954) 38–44 (especially 42–43)—an insight that strangely echoes Nietzsche's *Ein Buch für Alle und Keinen*. Though Eliot is primarily concerned with the dramatic voice, he does realize that difference between the voice of the poet talking to poet, or no one, and the way a poem behaves once in the hands of readers. A book can only perform for itself since it is impossible for the book to perform for readers. The elevation of a vocational academic book's narrative poetics—when a book's genre, audience, and voice align, when a book talks to itself—increases the chances that (i) an academic reader will experience the book left to right, and not merely consult as is so often the case; and (ii), ironically, non-academic readers, because they recognize the poetics of narrative, are far more likely

Notes

to travel along as *mythos* insists its *dianoia*. Poetics invites the many readers, ever so briefly and imperfectly, to desire, and then seek through reading, oneness with the book's one audience. • The poetic demands placed upon the narrative voice of the academic professional book, of necessity, render the narrator as reliable (as opposed to unreliable), as effectual (as opposed to omniscient or omnipotent), and invisible (and thus exclusively third, as opposed to first or second). Narrator reliability—simply a must if the academic book is to translate flesh and blood authorial expertise into flesh and blood readerly trust. At the point of reliability, implied author rests upon readerly perceptions of real author's expertise— and this despite claims for the complete effacement of the author (authors are merely and always readerly constructions), by Michel Foucault's "What is an Author?" in Donald F. Bouchard (ed.), *Language, Counter-Memory: Selected Essays and Interviews* (Ithaca: Cornell University Press, 1977) 113–38. To sustain narrative reliability the narrator must also tell a good tale. The narrator need not be omniscient, nor even can be, as shown by John Morreall, "The Myth of the Omniscient Narrator," *Journal of Aesthetics and Art Criticism* 52 (1994) 429–435. All that's required is that the story told be told well. The narrator of the vocational academic book exclusively speaks in the third person in order to weave a well-told story. To speak in any register other than the third person destroys the easy compact between voice, genre, and audience. Wayne Booth, *The Knowing Most Worth Doing: Essays on Pluralism, Ethics, and Religion* (Charlottesville: University of Virginia Press, 2010) 62–152 (the five essays that comprise part 2, Discerning Character in Criticism) demonstrates just how complicated narrative voicing can become when all three voices are in play. But beyond complications, the use of first and second person in an academic book is like the sneeze of an actor on stage: the fantastical is shattered into, the character dies, becoming a real person right before the eyes of the audience, who themselves scatter like freighted rabbits in their individual responses to the sneeze. This is why Christian Metz, *Film Language: A Semiotics of Cinema* (New York: Oxford University Press, 1974) 4, prefers the hermeneutical isolation of film—which mirrors the work of the invisible third in narrative—that can be completely and artistically controlled. The degree to which particularities of the author merge with the invisible, effectual, reliable narrator invites the many readers of the narratively structured vocational academic book to shed their own embedded particularities and jump the fence into the land of the book's one audience. • Traci C. West, *Wounds of the Spirit: Black Women, Violence, and Resistance Ethics* (New York: New York University Press, 1999) exemplifies the exception to the rule of the invisible third: West shows how the voice of the first person makes the personal experience a site of enquiry, a hermeneutical lens, and a purchase on justice. What is true for the study of the experience of Black women is equally true for all the forgotten, erased, marginalized, neglected, invisible, and oppressed. • What is true of the multiplicity of narrators (to use anything other than invisible third complicates and can even break the fiction so needed for narration) is equally true of quotations: quotations of anything other than primary sources introduces uncontrollable, unfocused, voices to the narration, and the attempt to characterize the many voices each time only heightens the narrative difficulties. While abundant in examples and smartly composed—and despite the size of the book and title it bears—Ruth Finigan's, *Why Do We Quote?: The Culture and History of Quotation* (Cambridge: Open Book Publishers, 2011) offers scant discussion for quotation's rationale (55–76), even if the consideration of the rhetorical effects of quotation more ample and sophisticated (183–97), though the use of Bakhtin to justify a text comprised of plural voices complicates, rather than solves, the question of effects for a vocational academic book. Terse, but inversely profitable, Eco's (*How to Write a Thesis* 156–67) "10 Rules" for quotation distinguishes between primary sources as objects of reflection and quotation—but even in this case in a qualified manner—and quotation's purpose as evidentiary. What winds up occupying sentence after sentence of prose should simply be relegated to the notes, where such in and out, give and take, good but not quite right, judgments belong. • The exception to the rule of quotation (only primary sources; never any secondary) is the quotation of contemporaries who have traditionally been excluded. Their quotations, and their names, should both be memorialized in the prose, regardless.

§ 8 Plot

The recapitulation of the way what has been discovered was discovered, while a tempting structuring strategy (and in truth one often followed by unreflective default), rarely reproduces in the re-telling the intrigue that first captured the noetic—thus proving an insufficient rhetorical device for the conversion of imagination. (Rarely does one noetic simply wish to tag along with another's journey.) The vocational academic book does narrate a story about what has been discovered, true enough; but it is not a replication of the act of discovery, nor a description and defense of the methods of discovery, nor even the history of research that frames, and even suggests, the path for discovery. The disambiguation of *discovery's* how from *telling's* how is what opens the door to the world of plotting for the academic professional book. • The five suggestive plots derive inductively from actual exemplars and are theoretically inspired by, grounded in, and loosely map to, the five codes Roland Barthes identifies in *S/Z: An Essay* (New York: Hill and Wang, 1974). Barthes himself privileges the hermeneutic (resolution of enigma) and proairetic (narrative of pure adventure), labeling them "irreversible codes" (codes that depend upon temporal sequence and thus must be read forward). Peter Brooks, *Reading for the Plot: Design and Intention in Narrative* (New York: Vintage, 1985) 18, 22–28, due to the coincidence of temporal and hermeneutic mechanics, claims the mystery story as narrative of all narratives. In the detective fiction, typified in Poe and Doyle, the hermeneutical "over codes" the proairetic. The fundamental "desire" of an academic book is to "explain" what has been only partially, or wrongly, understood. This insistence, this search for explanation, effectively over codes other plotting in the academic book, regardless of subgenre, be it a handbook, a textbook, a critical edition, a commentary, an encyclopedia. While this explanatory function is true of all books belonging in the academic phylum, the discourse of a narratively structured vocational academic book amplifies the role of such diagnosed confusion—the garbled, the odd, the ill-fitting, the absent, the distorted, the slough, the unclear, the bizarre, the incompatible—and makes confusion and absence the very point of departure. The vocational academic book begins its narrative discourse in the middle in its effort to explain the many impositions of just why it was that the dog did not bark. (For both Homer, *Odyssey* 16.1–15, and Holmes, *The Adventure of Silver Blaze,* canine silence occasions inferences that prove interpretively fruitful.) The bulk of discourse in an academic vocational book thus constitutes the transformation of an initial scene's disarray into a final scene's implications, a transformation enacted by the middle's heuristic, interpretive, and explanatory mechanics. The vocational academic book's metonymic movement forward between the two paired metaphors of introduction to conclusion—the first collapsed and marked by lack, the second, fully semiotic, marked by plentitude (Brooks, *Reading* 27)—can be traveled by a variety of plotted paths: by narrative action, by abductive repetition, by thick description, by taxonomic mapping and classification, or by selective episodic compounding. But plot picking is no mere menu ordering. Narration never so simple. The hermeneutical frame—from enigma to resolution—can find coherence in the juxtaposition of chapters that adhere to one, two, or even an assemblage of different possible plot structures. •

Notes

The ability for an abductive narrative frame for a vocational academic book to realize harmony among the potentially discordant parts that constitute the book's discursive middle not only resides in the primary aim of any academic book "to explain" but also in the very hermeneutics of abduction itself. Abduction's substitution of the coherent *for* the conflicted depends upon abduction's necessity to discover the coherent by first listening to the conflicted and then to reason backwards. Carlo Gizburg, "Clues: Roots of an Evidential Paradigm," in *Clues, Myths, and the Historical Method* (Baltimore: Johns Hopkins University Press, 1989) 96–125, shows how the trivial, the trifle, the smallest of detail, is that upon which the whole abductive act turns. The retracing of the armature of the oddities inherent to what's there (and the befuddlements of what should be or fairly expected but isn't) leads backwards to a coherent narrative that can explain the garbled discourse as it currently stands. Umberto Eco, "Horns, Hooves, and Insteps: Some Hypotheses on Three Types of Abduction" in Umberto Eco and Thomas A. Sebeok (eds.), *The Sign of Three: Dupin, Holmes, Peirce* (Bloomington: Indiana University Press, 1983) 198–220, not only roots abduction in Aristotle and Peirce, but refines the different types of abduction at work. The narratively structured academic vocational book practices "under coded abductions" (the preference of one hypothesis among several competitors) and/or "creative abduction" (the invention of a hypothesis *de novo*) in search of a totalizing "mega abduction" (an explanation that banishes all uncertainty). Thomas A. Sebeok, "One, Two, Three Spells U B E R T Y," in *Sign of Three* 1–10, shows that abduction commits the logical fallacy of affirming the consequent. The vocational academic book thus can only win hermeneutical triumph by making a sacrifice of permanence.

§ 9 Contents

Producing a table of contents is an exercise in list-making: the table inventories what comprises the finished book. As a representative catalogue, the table functions analogically and originates retrospectively. Only after the book is complete can the table be drawn to correspond. The hermeneutics thus run book to the table: the book imposes its will, dictating what can (only what's in) and should (never what's out) be listed. And many a table cast in such a mold— perfect impressions—rendered through obsessive numeric notation that visually marks descending and ascending relations. But the abundance of the merely analogical shutters. The profusion of denotative precision suffocates. Tables, when left to themselves, devolve to no more than rote, *post hoc*, memetic indexing. • Umberto Eco, *The Infinity of Lists* (New York: Rizzoli, 2009) 11–13, 113–16, characterizes such list-making as referential, finite, and unalterable, typified by Homer's description of Achilles' shield (*Iliad* 18.478–608). Eco contrasts Achilles' shield with Homer's listing of ships ready to set sail to Troy (*Iliad* 2.494–759) to suggest a second kind of list. The list of ships, Eco admits, is equally finite, equally mundane, equally referential, but their astronomical number speaks to the ineffable, the epic, the fantastical—not unlike the mythic work of biblical genealogies of Cain (Genesis 4:17–24), Seth (Genesis 5:1–22), Noah (Genesis 10:1–32), and even Jesus (Matthew 1:1–16; Luke 3:23–38), or the genealogies of the gods in Hesiod's *Theogony*. Such lists' inherent openness results in a kind of hermeneutical vertigo. A dizziness sets in, due to the list's size, obscurity, allusion, encryption, and tension (and outright contradictions). No mere inventory of what's present, such lists wrestle with what's not— Death and the Powers of the beyond. The finite list seeks to bring order to the disordered; but the infinite list admits the impossibility of bringing order, due to the recalcitrance of the disordered itself, which refuses easy and every imposition. Poetic lists acknowledge what's over the fence can never be named without remainder. Eco's poetic list echoes in the poetic table. • The poetic table sets the hermeneutical stakes high. The poetic table begs abduction. The naked table cries out for the imposition of that which organizes. The mystery surrounding the calculated selection and arrangement of a truncated number of items invites the search for a coherent explanation. The poetic table semiotically suggestive—never not analogically fixed. The innocent list, by disguise, craves an interpretive frame. • The poetic table generative, creating forward and not merely reflecting backward. The poetical table helps shape narration itself. The poetical table engages in hermeneutical conversation with text, from beginning right to the end. The lines of table, like those of verse, tested, abandoned, re-tried, fail, and then in a moment of revelation, capture both what has been and should be. The poetic table dabbles with the mysteries, the elements, the powers, that then dance with the gods across the pages. • The poetic table a *paidagogos* for reading. The poetic table guides. The poetic table teaches. The poetic table plots the journey. At the very moment the poetic table determines course, pointing to what's ahead, the poetic table equally tenders indetermined openness—as if to name an armada's every ship is to savor the whole of the grand journey upon which they will soon embark. • The poetic table enlists. Between table and text, between that which hints and that which unfolds, exists a vacuum. The gap between the poetic table's itinerary and the book's narrated journey engenders the desire for the journey. The absence between table and text elicits participation. The poetic table is not just a guide to what's to follow, though that it is. The poetic table beckons a visit to the world to follow. • Most tables content to keep good denotative company—wooden, prescriptive, memetic. The poetic table jumps the fence—and then bids all to follow suit.

§ 10 Sociology

Just how the confluence of three (some ancient) communal arrangements—the *collegium* (medieval craft guilds), the *societas* (the Enlightenment's professional academic societies), and the *ecclesia* (late antique and medieval church)—worked together in a fourth, the *universitas* (the natural extension of medieval monastic and cathedral schools) to foster a social context as homogenizing as totalizing for the contemporary noetic lingers, blissfully, just out of sight. • For the last 100 years, the American university has furnished the dedicated noetic with a fixed biographical pattern: apprenticeship (graduate school) that realizes its *telos* on a single day in a formal defense; for those upon whom Fortuna smiles, a seven-year, equally liminal, probationary period (assistant professor) follows apprenticeship, a period that itself culminates in an excruciating, rigorous "up or out" verdict (tenure); verdict's survival, at long last, grants security and begins an extended phase of self-regulating autonomy (associate professor), which is, finally and hopefully, crowned in the recognition of accomplishment, status, and influence (full professor). Though gnostic, byzantine, even secretive, the pattern neatly halves at tenure: all of apprenticeship and probation aims at it, and all noetic life to follow depends upon it. • This biographic arc did not arise *ex nihilo*. The progression of the noetic life from precarity (apprentice/assistant), through the grist mill of tenure, to security (associate/full) reflects the bipartite division of the medieval *studium* into *universitas magistrorum et scholarium*. The biographical arc of the contemporary noetic also eerily mirrors the patterned vocation that prevailed for workers in craft guilds for nearly 1,000 years—apprentice (for seven years)/journeyman [*sic*]/master—and equally recalls the progressive station points of *postulatum/novitius/monarchus* of monastic religious orders, station points that, as Peter Gemeinhardt, "In Search of Christian Paideia: Education and Conversion in Early Christian

Biography," *Zeitschrift für Antikes Christentum* 16 (2012) 88–98, shows, formalized in Christian paideia the ascetic practices stretching back to the fifth century. The structural similarities among university, guild, and church fails to surprise. The church gave birth to the university, and as its mother shaped its character, organization, and practices. Gary Richardson, "Craft Guilds and Christianity in Late-Medieval England: A Rational Choice Analysis," *Rationality and Society* 17 (2005) 139–189, shows that, not only were the naming of guilds, their structure, and the practices to be of Christian invention, but that both spiritual and economic aims reinforced each other in the guilds. Guild and university thus came by their professional biographical structures by honest ecclesial influence, even if tracing the lines proves far more serpentine and circuitous than direct. • Though the genetics of medieval arrangements still persist, the sociology of noetic progression in American universities developed in particularly American ways. America's antebellum universities took their early social cues from their venerable British and Scottish cousins: in residential settings, they sought to prepare (Protestant) clergy for the church and the elite for public service though the rote inculturation of the classics. But the resemblances end abruptly: American institutions answered to boards—comprised at first by clerics and then later dominated by magnates and tycoons—and not the Crown, boards whose intrusive rule meddled in every aspect of college life, including all matters of employment. The idea that teaching was a distinct profession, that faculty possessed rights, that research was part of the professorial charge, or that a college's fellows could exercise self-governance proved prepositus on American soil. • Between the Civil and Great wars American universities went to school in *Deutschland*. In the lecture halls of Halle, Göttingen, and Berlin they learned *Lehrfreiheit* (the self-regulating autonomy of the professor to teach what they deemed necessary and as they wished), *Lernfreiheit* (the self-regulating autonomy of the student, including non-university life), and *Freiheit der Wissenschaft* (the freedom to pursue pure research). As influential as these ideas were—though a good case can be made that they have been overly touted—the peculiarly American context refused their easy and wholesale transplanting. Lenore O'Boyle, "Learning for Its Own Sake: The German University as Nineteenth-Century Model," *Comparative Studies in Society and History* 25 (1983) 3–25, eloquently and thoroughly documents what did take root—the German de-coupling of education's direct service to church and civil service, freeing the ideal of "learning for learning's sake" to become a hallmark of professional identity for the American professor. • The period from the Great War to its Second witnessed the refiguring of the American university in distinctly American ways. The chief catalyst for transforming university teaching into a true profession was the work of a professional society. Professional societies, as Bernard Fay, "Learned Societies in Europe and America in the Eighteenth Century," *The American Historical Review* 37 (1932) 255–266, were children of the Enlightenment and, as such, were encyclopedic, even quixotic. North America's first academic professional society, the American Philosophical Society (1743), organized by Benjamin Franklin, embodied such a generalist vision. Slowly, over time, professional societies, particularly academic ones, consolidated and then reinforced professional identity through the ratcheting up of an ever-increasing disciplinary specialization. The formation of the American Association of University Professors (AAUP) in 1915 signaled that the professional identity of an academic professional had come of age, even if the specific triggering events for association's formation were narrowly legal. All that needs knowing about AAUP, especially its near scriptural, constitutional statements on tenure in 1915 and 1940, can be discovered in the magisterial work of Walter P. Metzger, e.g., "Academic Freedom and Scientific Freedom," *Daedalus* 107 (1978) 93–114. The AAUP's very existence and practices recognized a common sociology that transcended specific academic discipline and institutional type: a professor, any professor, every professor, belonged to the phylum of professors and shared a common biographical pattern with tenure as the narrative fulcrum whose possession underwrote security and academic freedom. Faculty were not employees but appointees, like federal judges, and, like judges, held the faculty of intellectual independence. Further, governing boards are agents of and must answer to public trust—and not merely to the fickle whims of a board's contemporary public, but to future publics as well. The AAUP legitimated the biographic arc of the noetic (the progression that establishes the professorial guild) and encoded tenure as the most important and powerful sign in the galaxy of signs comprising the university's universe (so, especially, O'Boyle, "Learning" 23 n64). • The book marks the successful transition at every stage in the noetic life. The would-be noetic begins in apprenticeship. Michel Foucault, *Discipline and Punish: The Birth of the Prison* (New York: Pantheon, 1977) 83, fingered apprentices as a potentially threatening class, though it turns out that noetic apprentices conform, and all too early and all too well, and as John Guillory points out, "Preprofessionalism: What Graduate Students Want," *Profession* (1996) 91–99. In apprenticeship the noetic acquires an academic field's necessary specialized knowledge, cultivates and refines the discrimination for handling acquired knowledge, and, most importantly, fosters a generative capacity for new discovery of new knowledge. This apprenticeship transpires under the close supervision of masters who model, advise, inspire, improve but, in the end, judge, a punctiliar judgment, rendered by a small group of masters, upon a single demonstration of knowledge, discrimination, and capacity in highly structured apprenticed long-form writing—the dissertation. Once apprenticeship complete, the probationary phase no longer requires close supervision, even if the now self-regulating noetic often benefits from assigned mentors and various progress reviews—all pitched as benevolent aids—before facing yet another critical judgment. The period of scrutiny, though, seems interminable, the formal procedure transpiring over months, even a year, and rendered by a much larger number of masters, externally solicited and internally *ex officio* at ever-escalating hierarchy. While a full dossier of professional accomplishments amassed during the probationary period supposedly forms the evidentiary basis for evaluation, again it is written work that forms the *de facto* primary means by which the noetic's future is determined—but this time a *body* of written work, and a body of *published* written work, a body of *peer-vetted* published work. The act of making public (publication), the amount of published writing (one book, two books, sometimes more), the perceived (borrowed) prestige of the publisher, and the documented impact of the body of work all figure the suitability of the noetic for approval. A noetic may discover salvation by faith, but tenure comes by books. • The successful survival brings the probationary period to an end for the noetic and rewards with provision of life-changing security and broad discretionary autonomy. It also inaugurates a long, indefinite, ill-defined period of journeying, during which the noetic, no longer bound by what must be written, becomes free to explore what can be written. The ambiguities of liberty can overwhelm; but freedom can equally unleash productivity. In either case, the noetic career always perceptually judged by books—by their number, their prestige, their impact. • The final stage recognizes the noetic as a master. The recognition ratified by formal institutional means and by the rendered esteem of peer members of the field's professional society. The legacy book can mark the move to master or can be the final jewel in the crown of a master's career. At every point, it is long-form written work, the book, that proves the measure of both social location, status, and advancement. • That the book formed the center of the university from its inception only betrays the book's centrality in the development of Christianity. Guy G.

Stroumsa, "The New Self and Reading Practices in Late Antique Christianity," *Church History and Religious Culture* 95 (2015) 1–18, documents how Christians capitalized upon the technology of the codex to make the Christian Bible, as well as its ancillary books, the catalyst for the project of Christian paideia that sought the transformation of the self, and not merely the cultivation of the self. Larry W. Hurtado, *Destroyer of the gods: Early Christian Distinctiveness in the Roman World* (Waco: Baylor University Press, 2016) 105–41, isolates Christianity's "bookishness" as a unique marker for the world's first transnational, transethnic religion. The book, by being the DNA code of Christianity, became essential to the genetic makeup of the university for 1,000 years.

• The book's continued role in the sociology of the noetic is threatened on two fronts: the complete transformation of academic life by the ebook and the rise of the corporate university. While the former can be dismissed with an easy urban "pft" (e has proven itself time and again a false messiah), it is the latter that is transforming the biography of noetic life and the book's centrality in the biography. The new corporate university is now governed by boards (and donors) who demand pragmatic results for their investments and have little patience for learning for learning's sake. The new corporate university now employs massive levels of a new management class whose sole task is to measure results. The new corporate university now insists faculty become economic engines in relentless pursuit of third-party funders who themselves expect specific results and dictate the terms and modes of dissemination. And the new corporate university, be it public or private, taking cues from for-profit institutions, is now systematically seeking to de-tenure (and thus de-professionalize) the professoriate through "adjunctification." The seeds for this massive transformation of the university were planted, and detectable, a decade ago, as chronicled by Frank Donoghue, *The Last Professors: The Corporate University and the Fate of the Humanities* (New York: Fordham University Press, 2008), and Ellen Schrecker, *The Lost Soul of Higher Education: Corporatization, the Assault on Academic Freedom, and End of the American University* (New York: The New Press, 2010). In the new corporate university, the complicated, byzantine sociology of the all-glorious, individuated, idiosyncratic noetic is coldly reduced to an economic pivot table.

§ 11 Social Psychology

While psychosocial human development theory has been applied to the life of the university student, in all of its dimensions, the life of the university professor has suffered a studied neglect. What led Jennifer A. Lindholm, "Pathways to the Professoriate: The Role of Self, Others, and Environment in Shaping Academic Career Aspirations," *The Journal of Higher Education* 75 (2004) 603–35, to observe that "very little theory or research, however, has focused specifically on the vocational development of college and university professors" (603) still holds two decades later: the social psychology of noetic life, from its mysterious beginnings, through its circuitous middle, right to its (often in-)glorious end, has yet to be researched, theorized, and written. What has been documented are the numberless issues faced when multiple sociological snapshots are taken of noetic life, as in Gretchen M. Bataille and Betsy E. Brown, *Faculty Career Paths: Multiple Routes to Academic Success and Satisfaction* (Westport, CT: Praeger, 2006) or Ginger Phillips MacDonald, "Theorizing University Identity Development: Multiple Perspectives and Common Goals," *Higher Education* 65 (2013) 153–166 (especially 157–60). Roger G. Baldwin and Robert T. Blackburn, "The Academic Career as a Developmental Process: Implications for Higher Education," *The Journal of Higher Education* 52 (1981) 598–614, come the closest to articulating psychosocial developmental theory for the noetic life (see, especially, 609, table 4). Although the lack of theory hampers, the empirical research into the social psychology of noetic life grounds two important observations: (i) the existing social locations of graduate student, assistant professor, associate professor, and full professor exert near totalizing valence; and (ii) the instrumentality of noetic productivity, measured in the number and quality of publications (especially the book), continues to be the means and mark for judging progression. • In the absence of empirical research and heuristic models, the work of Erik H. Erikson, *Childhood and Society* (New York: W. W. Norton & Company, 1963) 247–74, provides a suggestive social psychological frame for tracing the progression of the noetic and the instrumentality of the book within that progression. Erikson held that psychological development follows a lock-stepped course through eight (he later added a ninth) successive stages that stretch from infancy to adulthood. A crisis marks each stage, a crisis that could either help or hinder development: successful navigation of a stage's crisis results in the acquisition of an essential virtue, while failure stalls development and potentially compromises successful passage in other stages. • The particular utility of Erikson's theory resides in its attentiveness to the stages of development that mark adult life—and not (merely) a fixation upon the determinative events of infancy and early childhood. For Erikson, development as an adult proves as meaningful as that of childhood, making Erikson especially applicable for understanding the development of the noetic. Further, Erikson does not identify specific causes for successful navigation from stage to stage. This silence leaves room to isolate the book's pivotal role in the developmental life of the noetic. • The noetic passes through five discernably distinct psychological stages, with each stage featuring a psychological dilemma the noetic faces that comes by being in a new social location. Each stage also isolates the way the book proves instrumental to the acquisition of a stage's chief virtue and thus the successful navigation of the stage:

Stage	Psychosocial Dilemma	Social Setting	Social Instrument	Social Value
1	*insistency vs. indifference*	graduate school	dissertation	*achievement*
2	*recognition vs. invisibility*	professional guild	first book	*mattering*
3	*belonging vs. liminality*	beginning institution	tenure book	*security*
4	*vocation vs. careerism*	aspirational institution	vocational books	*congruence*
5	*generativity vs. stagnation*	elite group peers	legacy book	*permanence*

This theory of noetic development begs exegesis: (i) Stages 1–2, and sometimes even 3, can be compressed into a relatively short period of time—or they can be drawn out indefinitely, and painfully so. The variables impacting the length of time include both social location and the fact of a book. The noetic career often begins in a setting where writing is impossible, books are not valued, and security is not offered. It is nothing short of a tragic irony that the demands placed upon the noetic by the beginning institution deny the noetic the very means—books—that enable the transition to a setting that aligns more closely with noetic dreams. (ii) In stage 4 the noetic can choose to answer the threats of indifference (always a threat, regardless of stage), invisibility, and liminality with a competitive careerism. A book becomes just a(nother) way to get ahead, reducing writing to a transactional event that stifles the inner poet. (iii) This reading of the developmental path does not seek to homogenize experience. Women noetics, noetics of color, and LGBTQ noetics face unique, additional, and intersectional challenges. The strategies for overcoming such challenges include transforming genre to be a disruptive tool (rather than one that adheres to expectation) and to write the vocational book far earlier in one's noetic life—oftentimes even as the dissertation. The vocational and intentionally disruptive book triggers a far different set of dilemmas that are unique to those writing from the margins. (iv) Nor does the model seek to gloss over new corporate university practices of "adjunct-ification," (the reduction of tenured lines in favor of part-time, clinical, non-tenured posts), "STEM-ification," (the de-emphasis of the liberal arts in favor high impact–factor scientific research), and "revenue-ification" (the de-emphasis of research for research's sake in favor of research that secures third-party funding that turns faculty into economic engines). Despite faculty diversity and university transformation, the contemporary noetic still faces a series of common and predictable psychosocial developmental dilemmas resolved, astoundingly, through publication and, particularly, the book.

§ 12 Editors

The attempt to explain "who editors *are*" naturally defaults to "what editors *do*." But a list of tasks that editors regularly perform, helpful though it is, does not account for their enigmatic nature and ways, let alone reveal the ancient origins and mythic meaning of their work. Editors perform similar tasks regardless of book, discipline, author, publisher, or even the pronounced eccentricities of a particular editor. Given that editors pretty much do the same tasks prompted Ingo von Münch and Georg Siebeck, *Der Autor und sein Verlag* (Tübingen: Mohr Siebeck, 2013) to tackle the question of editorial identity by examining the philosophical underpinnings of both authors and editors and to do so inside the author–editor relationship created by the act of publishing a book. Münch and Siebeck show just how uneven, asymmetrical, and profoundly nuanced the author–editor relationship really is. It takes considerable effort to reduce the author–editor relationship to something that is purely transactional, but obsessive quest for money is able to do just that. • The power disparity between the noetic publisher and the noetic threatens to scuttle the collegial author–editor relationship before it can be established. Although laser focused on the ethically fraught world of (mainly STEM) journal articles—and thus not on HSS books *per se*—the essays comprising Ciaran Sugrue and Sefika Mertkan's (eds.) *Publishing and the Academic World: Passion, Purpose and Possible Futures* (London: Routledge 2016) do finger the raft of ethical problems surrounding academic publishing's historic concentration in the global north. But the impositions of geography (and thus equally of the English language) are not the only systemic power imbalances requiring interrogation. The collection of essays gathered by Savva, Maria, and Lynn P. Nygaard (eds.), *Becoming a Scholar: Cross-Cultural Reflections on Identity and Agency in an Education Doctorate* (London: University College of London Press, 2021) points to how the intersectionality of race, gender, and being a first-generation PhD reveals that many authors lack the required cultural capital to navigate publishing and to understand editors. This depravation of capital makes the author–editor relationship decidedly one-sided. The political and economic mechanics of what's blithely taken for granted—e.g., proposals, peer reviews, approval committees, not to mention the complexities of copyright and contracts—can baffle junior and senior alike, but such "assumed" knowledge places those lacking cultural capital in significant disadvantage to publisher and thus editor. Because systemic power dynamics go unnamed, unexamined, and undiscussed, achieving trust and mutuality between author and editor borders on the miraculous. That authors and editors do so often beat the odds and wind up fostering a genuine partnership owes not only to their respective goodwill but, equally, to the book's sacramental power to bind the many differences of two as a held-in-common one. • Editors, initially or before otherwise introduced, are often conceived, like some distant deity, as impersonal and unknowable. And with good reason. Notoriously elusive, often enigmatic, their world mysterious (and its zero-sum complexities little appreciated), work magical (exactly how they improve a book bewilders), temperaments mercurial (and often disparaged), and identities strategically cloaked (access funneled into the anonymous with submission instructions as inviting as a "no trespassing" warning). Stephen McGinty, *Gatekeepers of Knowledge: Journal Editors in the Sciences and the Social Sciences* (Westport, CT: Bergin & Garvey, 1999), drawing upon the sociology of Kurt Lewin and the mythology of Joseph Campbell, rightly casts the author as the hero, the protagonist in their own noetic narrative, and positions the editor in equally mythic terms as an "elder"—a wise helper, who already knows the way whom the hero must consult. Michael A. Pemberton, "Gatekeeper, Guardian, or Guide: Negotiating the Dynamics of Power as an Editor," in Greg Giberson, Megan Schoen, and Christian Weisser (eds.), *Behind the Curtain of Scholarly Publishing: Editors in Writing Studies* (Boulder: University Press of Colorado, 2022) 139–52 (especially 144–47), pushes McGinty's use of a mythic trope even further: editors are divine guardians of the threshold, alternatively enabling or preventing the noetic hero's passage. This power, this wisdom, this competency, this experientially based instinct, is what William Germano calls *Fingerspitzengefühl*, in a book that can only be understood as required scriptural reading for any would-be noetic, *Getting It Published: A Guide for Scholars and Anyone Else Serious about Serious Books*, 3rd ed. (Chicago: University of Chicago Press, 2016) 90–91. This "fingertip feeling" points to the editor's almost god-like ability to size up author and book instantly, an augury that authors find hard to believe and harder still to accept when experienced. • Editors' numinous capacity, their almost sacred roles, and their strategic cloaking encourage their noetic stereotyping as perpetually aloof. The easy breezy blunder is to assume editors blaze, indifferent, unmoved. Not so. Far from it, despite the many well-curated cool personas. Editors are the ever-assiduous, enterprising, relentless instigators—the full orbit of which Gregory M. Britton captures in "Thinking Like a Scholarly Editor: The How and Why of Academic Publishing," in Peter Gina (ed.), *What Editors Do: The Art, Craft, and Business of Book Editing* (Chicago: University of Chicago Press, 2017) 40–48. The editor's waking hours get spent in self-motivated dreaming, planning, looking, wishing, wanting, assessing, hoping, seeking, a fact that surprises the fearful novice and jaded senior alike. For the editor, the possibility of the next book always coveted as much as the taste of the last still savored. The intentional editorial search for authors mirrors the authorial search for editors and this opens the door to collaboration. • Instigator a primary descriptor, but not an exhaustive one. An editor equally a mediary, a practiced go-between, a shrewd plenipotentiary, a publisher's ambassador, an author's diplomat. Even if paid by the publisher, the editor always seeks faithful representation of the one to the other. The editor stands with both author and publisher simultaneously. The editor's discriminated administration of power—bequeathing the almighty yes, rendering the devastating no—must balance the embedded asymmetrical politics and dispiriting economics of the publisher with the realities and hopes of the noetic, all teetering upon the tiniest precipice where judged merit and conjured potential impact meet. Always a mediator, the editor must be a spell-casting sorcerer to the house and a truth-telling prophet to the noetic. • That author and editor share so many of the same concerns makes the alliance possible. The two both care. A midwife—to nurture, coach, educate, effect; to be present, to make the often painful bearable, to inspire fortitude, to give hope. An editor shares the author's dreams for the book and does everything possible to help each author realize those dreams in and by the book. While each experience is different, unique, singular—no two books or authors alike—each instance profits from the rich deposit of an editor's hard-won wisdom. Sharing the book—from acquisition and development, through publication, to its life in the world—builds a bond between author and editor. • Author and editor, editor and author, a confection made of bookish dreams.

§ 13 Presses

The problem hermeneutical. The dream of discovering *an* appropriate publisher, let alone *the* perfect publisher, turns into a nightmare. While publishers are well practiced at discerning which potential projects fit their publishing aims, the noetic is not. Even the well-seasoned struggles to "read" presses for fit. The clear-eyed, succinct, and clarifying guidance about what distinguishes publisher from publisher that Beth Luey provides in her *Handbook for Academic Authors*, 4th ed. (Cambridge: Cambridge University Press, 2002) 46–60, or what Paul Parsons gives in his dated but still instructive and relevant, "Specialization by University Presses," *Book Research Quarterly* 6 (1990) 3–15, fail to account for the host of unknowns bedeviling the right alignment of noetic book with noetic publisher. Success requires the marriage of the complicated social, psychological, and semiotic world of the noetic to the publisher's precise mix of money, mission, and prestige. The noetic must possess, on the one hand, noetic self-awareness, institutional savvy, and astute professional politic and, on the other hand, broad publishing industry acumen and specific publisher knowledge. Bereft of both the noetic easily becomes perplexed, even paralyzed, and succumbs to colophon hypnosis (mesmerized by what's on the spine with all hope pinned to the supposedly superior two or three) or surrenders to pragmatic diffidence (whoever agrees first is just fine). The result all too often disappointment—and some embarrassment—when rejection occurs or frustration when noetic and publisher aims are discovered not to align. • The problem hermeneutical. No single publisher attribute tells the whole tale; it is always, and only, in combination that publisher traits pixilate enough to provide the cues so necessary for noetic decisions. Even so, misreading the various traits, individually and collectively, occurs, as what regularly circulates in the noetic world as urban legend provides a contradictory wisdom about the proper valence of publisher characteristics. What fascinates, and equally perplexes, is that a case can be made for almost any permutation of the conjectured affordances.

Publisher Trait	Conjectured Affordance
Size	Bigger presses are better, as a single volume is carried along by the larger list.
	Smaller presses are better, as a single volume can receive specialized attention.
Age	Historic presses are better because their claims upon legacy instantly bequeath social and political capital to the book and author.
	Younger presses are better because they cannot afford complacency and translate their youth into relentless effort for their books and authors.
Ownership	Corporate presses are better, as they place a premium on profit and thus will always engage in aggressive and sometimes expensive marketing and sales efforts.
	Nonprofit presses are better, as they place a premium on mission and will always make sure the book gets to those who need it most at an affordable price.
Scope	Presses that publish in multiple disciplines and serve multiple professional societies are better because a book has the chance to reach more readers.
	Presses that who concentrate on just one discipline and one professional society are better because the press can forge a set of readers who come to expect relevant books year after year.

Notes 121

Selectivity	The restrictive presses, with their stringent and selective approval processes, are better in that they guarantee the much-coveted respect from peers and exposure in the premier journals.
	The populist presses are better because their willingness to take risk, to break with norms, and to publish the disruptive and non-canonical.
Editorial Intervention	A "brokerage" press, where editors simply hand off to production what is received, is better because it ensures that the book will publish just as written and wanted.
	An "artisan" press, where editors spend enormous sums of time developing project, ensures that the published book will be all it could and should be.
Production Values	"Assembly line" presses whose process routinized, automated even, are better because they will always realize a physical book within the standard deviation, even if the end product is more disposable than durable.
	"Artifact" presses whose process is built from the ground up with each book are better because they craft a durable physical book as distinctive as its ideas.
Market Focus	Presses that publish for academic, professional, and trade markets (or just trade markets) in equal measure—often requiring an agent—are better because they know how to take an academic book and help it reach the widest number of readers.
	Presses that publish for only academic markets are better because the chance for noetic disappointment decreases because publisher and market are aligned.

Other publisher traits—required author subventions, publisher cultural, ethical, or community partisanship—that regularly form grist for noetic coffee pot conversations only muddy the waters further. • The problem hermeneutical. No quick and easy resolution presents itself. One noetic option inductive, rooted in the inferences derived from a simple survey of the number of times a particular publisher appears in the critical literature enshrined in a work's notes. But inductive subject matter alignment does not account for all publisher intangibles. The other option abductive, rooted in a far more difficult and less precise imaginative act. This option asks the noetic to expend serious effort in examining the long history of a publisher's books in the attempt to work backwards from list after list to the story a publisher is attempting to tell. As Roberto Calasso argues, *Art of the Publisher* 11–12, a publisher's list of published works implies a narrative coherence. This narrative coherence may be the single best guide for the perplexed noetic in search of alignment with a publisher. • But the problem more than hermeneutical. Paige Mann, "Scholarship in a Globalized World: The Publishing Ecosystem and Alternatives to the Oligopoly," in Abby Day, Lois Lee, Dave S.P. Thomas, and James Spickard (eds.), *Diversity, Inclusion, and Decolonization: Practical Tools for Improving Teaching, Research, and Scholarship* (Bristol: Bristol University Press, 2022) 186–202, identifies the disturbing corporate context for most noetic publishing (and offers helpful paths of resistance), while Patricia H. Thornton and William Ocasio, "Institutional Logics and the Historical Contingency of Power in Organizations: Executive Succession in the Higher Education Publishing Industry, 1958–1990," *American Journal of Sociology* 105 (1999) 801–43, identify the insular ways power distributes within the noetic publishers, and Elea Gimenez-Toledo, Jorge Mañana-Rodrıguez, and Gunnar Sivertsen, "Scholarly Book Publishing: Its Information Sources for Evaluation in the Social Sciences and Humanities," *Research Evaluation* 26 (2017) 91–101, pull the curtain back on the problems inherent to prestige rankings of noetic publishers.

§ 14 Mythology

In many justifiable ways, this particular section as well as all the others, owes to the confluence of Calasso's belief in the power of the book to transport, the power of what can be discovered when conveyed, what J. R. R. Tolkien, "On Fairy-Stories" in *Tree and Leaf* (Boston: Houghton Mifflin, 1965) 3–73, calls the "secondary" world. This section, as well as all the others, equally depends upon the scandal of particularity—that book's flawed glory lives in its incarnational singularity.